Teaching
Diverse
Learners

To Chad,
With gratitude for your unconditional love, support, and generosity of spirit,
And to James, Claire, and Katie, who never cease to amaze and inspire

To my parents, Jeanne and Harry Mazur, who taught me to cherish diversity,
And to my children Arin and Adam, who share in the joy of the diversity of our lives

And to our students,
Who constantly inspire us with their tireless efforts to nurture and support their own students

Teaching
Diverse
Learners

Principles for
Best Practice

Amy J. Mazur
Patricia Rice Doran

CORWIN

A SAGE Company

For information:

Corwin
A SAGE Company
2455 Teller Road
Thousand Oaks, California 91320
(800) 233-9936
Fax: (800) 417-2466
www.corwin.com

SAGE Ltd.
1 Oliver's Yard
55 City Road
London EC1Y 1SP
United Kingdom

SAGE India Pvt. Ltd.
B 1/I 1 Mohan Cooperative
    Industrial Area
Mathura Road, New Delhi 110 044
India

SAGE Asia-Pacific Pte. Ltd.
33 Pekin Street #02-01
Far East Square
Singapore 048763

Printed in the United States of America.

Library of Congress Cataloging-in-Publication Data

Mazur, Amy J.
Teaching diverse learners: principles for best practice / Amy J. Mazur, Patricia Rice Doran.
    p. cm.
Includes bibliographical references and index.
ISBN 978-1-4129-7498-1 (pbk.)
   1. Inclusive education—United States. 2. Educational equalization—United States.
3. Children with social disabilities—Education—United States. I. Doran, Patricia Rice. II. Title.

LC1201.M375 2010
379.2'60973—dc22   2010023534

This book is printed on acid-free paper.

10   11   12   13   14   10   9   8   7   6   5   4   3   2   1

Acquisitions Editor:	Jessica Allan
Associate Editor:	Joanna Coelho
Editorial Assistant:	Allison Scott
Production Editor:	Cassandra Margaret Seibel
Copy Editor:	Cynthia Long
Typesetter:	C&M Digitals (P) Ltd.
Proofreader:	Susan Schon
Indexer:	Jean Casalegno
Cover Designer:	Karine Hovsepian

Contents

Acknowledgments

This book would not have been possible without the support of many individuals. First, we appreciate the competent and collaborative support we have received from Corwin; particularly from our editors, David Chao and Jessica Allan; and our editorial assistants, Allison Scott, Brynn Saito, and Sarah Bartlett; as well as our copy editor, Cynthia Long, and our production editor, Cassandra Seibel. We appreciate, also, the assistance we have received from our colleagues in the bilingual special education program at the George Washington University, especially Tara Courchaine, Liz Crouch, Meghan Mulhern, Allison Neaves, and Marly Reed. Numerous times, they made suggestions or pointed out concepts that have found their way into this book, and we are grateful for their continued willingness to share ideas as well as to provide many photographs for use in the manuscript. In the same way, our own students—as well as various K–12 students and their family members—have been a constant source of inspiration to us, continuously providing us with new ideas and innovative approaches to challenges they may face. We are particularly grateful to the following individuals, who graciously allowed us to use their visual likenesses or to quote from their work: Meredith Alexander, Maurice Ambe, Divine Anjeh, Lorrie Armfield, Melody Brooks, Aranda Brown, Lori Crawford, Elizabeth Crouch, Catherine Doran, Claire Doran, James Doran, Michelene Evans, Josh Fine, Dana Hassan, Mahmoud al-Hassan, Wafa Hassan, Nestor Hurtado, Graham Jardines, Teresa Jardines, Betsy Johnson, Kevin Kendrick, Adam Liberman, Arin Liberman, Christine Mann, Courtney Mason, Jeanne Mazur-Messing, Stacie Morton-Carter, Mark Moser, Meghan Mulhern, Fatima Nacaytuna, Allison Neaves, Carmen Parada, Cristian Parada, Patricia Parada, Elise Rebhorn, Theresa Rebhorn, Jung-A Seo, Ayana Shabazz, Albert Spencer, Janet Spencer, Dayna Stropkay, Jennifer Wingate, and June Zillich.

Finally, to our families, who made it possible for us to dedicate months to this manuscript, thank you for your help and tireless support of this project. To Chad Doran, whose comments and critiques in the early stages of this project were invaluable, we extend a special note of gratitude and appreciation.

About the Authors

 **Amy J. Mazur,** EdD, lead faculty in bilingual special education and a professor at the George Washington University, has been involved in teacher preparation for over 30 years. She has long been an advocate for the minority student who, as a result of poverty, health and developmental issues, immigrant status, or level of English language acquisition, has not been provided access to appropriate educational service delivery. Dr. Mazur has served as the chair of the Special Education Special Interest Group of the National Association for Bilingual Education (NABE); and she has been a member of the editorial staff of the Division for Culturally and Linguistically Diverse Exceptional Learners (DDEL), a division of the Council for Exceptional Children. Throughout her career, Dr. Mazur has presented at national and international conferences, advocating for the rights of minority students as well as the skills needed to prepare professionals to teach to the needs of all students. She lives in Washington, D.C., and is the mother of two children, Arin and Adam, both of whom have been an inspiration to her as she seeks to promote social justice and equity.

 **Patricia Rice Doran,** MA is a project director for a federally funded teacher training program at the George Washington University, which provides professional development for general educators working with culturally and linguistically diverse students. She has taught graduate-level teacher education courses focused on topics of special education, ESOL, and literacy and has presented at numerous conferences as well. She has worked with culturally and linguistically diverse student populations as a general and special educator in both public and private educational settings. She serves as the co-chair of the Special Education Special Interest Group for the National Association for Bilingual Education (NABE). She lives in Baltimore with her husband Chad and their three children, James, Claire, and Katie.

Introduction

You may be approaching this text with the hope of finding the one simple answer or easy trick for teaching diverse learners. Like many teachers in today's educational world, you may have been disappointed because there is not a clear answer that works every time, for every student, from every background, in every school. Diversity comes in many forms. There is no one set of strategies, assessments, or accommodations that will enable every student always to be successful in the school environment. However, we believe there is a framework that may help you to ask the right questions, reflecting on your students, their backgrounds, and the instructional methods and assessments you use. It is our goal to present some crucial elements of that framework and to make them accessible and relevant to your classroom.

This book has two goals. The first is to allow you to examine your current repertoire of skills regarding instruction, assessment, and adaptations. Whether a new teacher or an accomplished and experienced veteran, each of us is constantly working to improve our practice in light of the changes that we see every year as communities, demographics, and populations change. These changes may present new challenges and require us to stretch our teaching repertoire in ways we might never have anticipated.

Equally important, the second goal of this book is to function as a guidebook to help you learn what important issues are most relevant to instruction of diverse learners and how best to acquire competency in those areas. To this end, the book addresses topics such as recent law and policy changes, cultural issues relevant to immigration, the process of acquiring a second language and the impact of that process on students' academic and social well-being, definitions of second-language acquisition, language difference and disability, and accommodations and modifications for students with special education needs or those in the process of second-language acquisition.

The upside of the challenges facing classroom teachers, of course, is that in reality we are not working "without assistance." Social and demographic changes, coupled with recent policy mandates, require all teachers to be aware of the needs of all students. However, those changes have also created a school climate where collaboration is encouraged. None of us works alone; in reality, many school professionals have complementary skill sets, and the most complete information possible can be gained when we work together. Imagine a situation where a third-grade student is having trouble in a reading lesson: The classroom teacher speaks to the reading teacher, speaks to the special educator, and recommends that the special education referral process begin as soon as possible, so the student can be diagnosed and supported appropriately. Compare that process, with two or three professionals sharing information, with the following: The reading teacher sits down with the speech and language professional, the special educator, the classroom teacher, and the guidance counselor—all together in the same room at the same time—to identify the issues and craft a prereferral intervention that addresses all relevant factors impacting the student's performance. One could reasonably expect the second approach to be dramatically more successful. It is even more important for classroom teachers, faced with increasing pressure in this era of accountability and reform, to find support through their colleagues. This book is an effort to support you in identifying those within your building who might be the best, most effective sources of information and support, and to assist you in finding effective ways to move forward in collaborating with them for student success.

WHO SHOULD USE THIS BOOK

Increasingly, the responsibility of serving diverse learners falls not on "special" teachers or "special" programs. The twin national mandates of the Individuals With Disabilities Education Act (IDEA), which mandates placement in the "least restrictive environment" appropriate for students with disabilities, and the No Child Left Behind (NCLB) Act, which evaluates schools based on all students' accomplishment of content objectives, required schools to incorporate diverse learners into general education classrooms and to focus on their achievement and progress once there. We strongly believe this change is a positive one; however, we also believe that inclusive programs demand adequate teacher support, awareness, and training. Inclusion without appropriate resources and collaborative practice is unfair to teachers and students alike. Therefore, we believe strongly that all teachers, including and especially general educators, must be aware of the skills and background knowledge needed to meet the students' needs. This book is designed for any classroom professional currently working with—or interested in learning how to work with—diverse learners: students with disabilities, English language learners (ELLs), students from minority populations, and so on.

HOW TO USE THIS BOOK

We suggest that you use this book in a "both-and" kind of way: both as a practical guidebook and as an aid to reflective practice. One tenet of effective instruction is the value and importance of reflection and self-evaluation. According to Paolo Freire (1993), a Brazilian educator renowned for his contributions to the fields of both education and social justice, education "bases itself on creativity and stimulates true reflection . . . upon reality" because we meet our potential only through "inquiry" and "creative transformation" (p. 84). In other words, it is only through thinking about, and evaluating, what we do that we are able to consider what worked, what did not work, and what we can change, improve, or develop anew.

| Figure 0.1 | Eight Ways to Use This Book in Professional Growth |

Even those of us who have years of experience are challenged to continue growing professionally and, often, to document that growth in professional portfolios, growth logs, and observations. Below are some suggestions for using the tools provided in this book for your own professional growth:

1. Begin a discussion group with colleagues on the chapter topics.

2. Summarize and present chapters at staff development meetings.

3. Read, reflect, and write on your own.

4. Complete the action steps listed at the end of each chapter, and include the results in your professional growth plan.

5. Summarize essential points from one or two chapters to provide a "guide" for colleagues.

6. Make an appointment with a colleague to plan together using suggestions from each chapter.

7. Meet with your school's instructional intervention team to generate a list of recommended general education interventions and adaptations.

8. Select a student or preservice teacher in your building and meet regularly with that individual to review particular chapters.

Figure 0.1 includes a number of suggestions for using this book for your own professional growth and for supporting change in your professional community. You can use this book on your own as a self-study activity as well: Reflective questions and activities are provided at the end of each chapter for that purpose.

1 Who Are Our Diverse Learners?

New Definitions, New Responses

The first staff meeting of the year used to be a time for reunions, catching up with colleagues after 10 relaxing weeks, and sharing enthusiasm for the new year. Over the past three years, the first days of school had become increasingly tension filled for teachers at Glendale Middle School. These days would typically bring news of how the school's student body—a diverse group who hailed from more than 80 countries, had various disabilities, and was overwhelmingly eligible for free and reduced-price meals—had done on the state's exam. For the last two years, Glendale had failed to make adequate yearly progress (AYP). As the principal stated to a somber group at this year's meeting, this upcoming year would "make or break" them. If the students failed to make AYP (in all subgroups, including special education, students receiving free and reduced-price meals, and English language learners [ELLs]), then the school would go into corrective action and could even, down the road, be selected for restructuring. The principal—whose own job was on the line—ended by urging teachers to redouble their efforts, doing whatever was necessary to ensure that every student passed the state's proficiency test.

As she walked out of the meeting, Katrina, a first-year teacher, felt apprehensive and turned to Roberto, a veteran who was widely regarded as a competent teacher respected by the students. "What do you think of this?" she asked. Roberto shook his head. "All those people who make policy . . . don't they know what kind of students we have?" he said. "I love these kids. I think they're amazing. But they're never going to read and do math as well as kids from the other side of town. That's the hand we've been dealt. When will those people at the state board of ed. realize that?"

THE ISSUES

- Teacher preconceptions of students' abilities
- Increasing diversity in student populations
- Increased pressure on teachers to ensure all students achieve
- Ability of teachers to identify and respond to diverse student needs

QUESTIONS TO CONSIDER

1. What new challenges do the changing demographics of Glendale Middle present to the school's teachers?

2. How can teachers at Glendale provide support to scaffold successful test performance for a diverse student body?

3. What specific factors (cultural differences, language proficiency, family issues, community challenges, etc.) are limiting the achievement of students at Glendale?

4. How can teachers at Glendale adapt and change their instructional approaches to respond to those specific factors?

5. How does Roberto's preconception of his students impact his ability to reach those students?

GETTING THE ANSWERS

Although fictional, this scene is representative of much of what occurs at schools across the country in teachers' first weeks back to school. Increasingly, the trend toward accountability has put teachers and administrators under pressure to raise test scores, at any and all costs. Teachers are being challenged to target all students, to retool their approaches to ensure that all students are learning, and to reevaluate their own established practices in the process. All of this, to some degree, is good, as it ensures that teachers will continue to pay attention to all students. However, the challenge for teachers lies in reconciling the push toward testing proficiency with a true reflective approach to teaching—while still maintaining a willingness to teach beyond the test; to try whatever is needed to help students achieve; and to assess students in a manner appropriate to their culture, language background, skills, and abilities.

Teachers increasingly must master a variety of skills and must be familiar with current research on diversity, language, and differentiated instruction.

These two goals may seem incompatible, but they are both inescapably part of the post-NCLB landscape in America.

We believe that true reflective teaching is essential to reach students and to transform their lives—and that reflection is not something abstract or apart from the classroom. Rather, reflection is a process that must be deeply connected to the classroom and must occur within it—as we look out at our students, survey their accomplishments, examine the roadblocks they encounter, and think about what we might change. Throughout this book, we model that process of reflection, with aids and activities designed to help you reevaluate the issues and dynamics of your classroom and the effectiveness of particular approaches and strategies.

For teachers at schools like Glendale, the challenge lies in finding a way to identify the increasingly diverse needs of the student population, so as to begin addressing those needs in the classroom. This can be a complex process: Our schools have increasing numbers of English language learners; students with special education needs; students who are commonly considered at risk due to any one of several factors (such as poverty or socioeconomic disadvantage); and students who may fall into one, two, or all of those groups. These are referred to as "triple-threat" students (Rueda & Chan, 1979). To identify students' needs and appropriate strategies to meet those needs, the teacher must first identify what type of prior knowledge and skill set students bring to the classroom. The students, for their part, must figure out how prior knowledge and prior experiences relate to the classroom demands encountered in school. Often, for the students, this task is overwhelming, as they struggle to figure out classroom expectations, use of academic language, nonverbal communication, cultural and pragmatic norms, the literal and behavioral language of the classroom, policies, and procedures while also struggling to master academic content. The onus is often placed on students to determine how to negotiate complex classroom and school questions while also attempting to master curriculum.

The questions in Figure 1.1 are faced on a daily basis by a growing population of students, who must navigate their way through the complex academic, social, and emotional issues that are part of any child's educational process. In fact, the phenomenon of students bearing greater responsibility for their own acculturation into school has become more common as the number of diverse learners in our school continues to increase. As our national demographics change and our society becomes more diverse, so too do our schools and classrooms change. Since 1991, in fact, the population of school-age ELLs nationally has increased over 100% (Kindler, 2002). In other words, across the nation we have seen our English language learner population more than double—and some areas have experienced far more dramatic growth. Twenty-four states currently count ELL students as 5% or more of their general student population—a statistic which, if extrapolated to the classroom level, indicates that in a classroom of 20 students, at least one, and probably more, will not have English as a primary language. In the states with the highest concentration of ELLs, the percentage is much higher than that average indicates (National Clearinghouse for English Language Acquisition, 2008). Of these ELL students, it can be assumed that 10% to 12%, like the general U.S. population, may

Figure 1.1	Questions Culturally and Linguistically Diverse (CLD) Students Face

For a CLD student, the process of becoming used to school procedures and environments can be overwhelming. Before even confronting the question of mastering content, this student may be confronted with various other complex questions, the answers to which are implicit but may not ever be explicitly taught:

How do I order lunch?

What materials can I take home?

What materials are "mine" as opposed to "ours" and "shared"?

Where do I get my books?

When can I talk to my neighbor: When is it "working together" and when is it "misbehaving"?

Where should I sit? Can I sit next to others? Where do I keep my things?

Can I use the restroom at school? Do I need to ask for permission to do so?

What emotions can I show, and when?

Can I ask for help? How? Who can help me?

What if I don't know how to ask for what I need?

What if I don't know what I need?

What if no one else understands the language I am speaking?

What if I don't feel safe?

require special education services (U.S. Department of Education, 2008), and certainly require informed, linguistically appropriate assessment to determine their eligibility for services (Hoover, Klingner, Baca, & Patton, 2008). All of these changes mean that general educators, who used to be assured of a fairly homogenous class, now find themselves in the role of ESOL (English for speakers of other languages) teacher, reading specialist, counselor, special educator, and so on. Therefore, educators increasingly need to expand their skill sets, using a variety of strategies to meet the needs of culturally and linguistically diverse exceptional (CLD/E) learners, including ELLs with or without disabilities as well as all students with special education needs, and other students—and to effectively differentiate among all of those needs. This process begins with an accurate understanding of who your students really are—what backgrounds they have, what prior experiences and knowledge they bring, and what type of family situations they go home to each evening.

This process also involves an awareness of the impact that factors such as cultural diversity, changing cultural norms, family trauma and emotional adjustment, and second-language acquisition can have on learning. Figure 1.2 describes some of the expectations that may be challenging for ELL students—though our schools are set up to take them for granted. Cummins (2007) describes the process of second-language acquisition, pointing out that students can acquire basic interpersonal communicative skills (BICS) in one to three years, but they typically need five to seven years, and sometimes up to ten years, to master academic language (cognitive academic language proficiency, or CALP).

Figure 1.2	Hidden Demands of Cognitive Academic Language Proficiency (CALP)

Many of the linguistic demands we place on students actually may require more-advanced language proficiency skills than we realize. The ability to use academic English becomes a prerequisite for understanding, as students cannot comprehend a text without understanding these crucial words. The following list highlights 10 common academic keywords that may be challenging to ELL students, with or without disabilities. The language and content demands of your classroom may vary; you may wish to skim the textbooks and materials you use to see what other academic words are prerequisites for understanding.

Above

Below

Beyond

Behind

In Front of, Before, Preceding

Different

Same, Similar

Compare

Contrast

Within

NEW STEPS TO TAKE—TOMORROW

We don't actually advocate trying all of these new steps in one day. However, we do recommend making a deliberate commitment to engage in Freire's (1993) type of reflection—reflective activity connected to the classroom and occurring inside the classroom rather than separate and away from it. In this section, you'll see some suggestions, tips, and charts that you can begin to use immediately in order to get to know your students better.

1. Consider your classroom: Who are your students?

In addition to understanding your own perceptions and attitudes, it is helpful to understand your classroom demographics and dynamics—and how they relate to national or schoolwide norms. As much of our social discourse is based on traditional labels designed around concepts such as ethnicity, cultural identity, and ability, we include charts based on traditional categories—but we also encourage you to think outside the box and chart your own categories here, defining your students in ways other than the traditional deficit-based ones.

Complete the tables in Figures 1.3 and 1.4 to compare your school and classroom demographics to national norms. Figure 1.3 prompts you to think through the cultural and ethnic diversity of your school and your classroom as they relate to national trends. Figure 1.4 provides a space to record the diversity of educational and etiological needs (related to a particular condition or set of symptoms) in your school and classroom.

| Figure 1.3 | Cultural and Ethnic Diversity in Your Classroom and School |

	Nationally (as Percentage of Total Student Enrollment)	In My School	In My Classroom
Caucasian	66.9		
African American	12.3		
Latino, Hispanic	14.4		
Asian, Pacific Islander	4.3		
Native American, Alaskan, Hawaiian	0.8		
Other or more than one race	1.3		

Source: U.S. Department of Education, National Center for Educational Statistics (2008).

| Figure 1.4 | Continuum of Needs in Your Classroom and School |

	Nationally (as Percentage of Total Student Enrollment)	In My School	In My Classroom
Specific learning disability	5.8		
Autism spectrum disorder, developmental delay	1.0		
Hearing, vision, speech, and language impairment	3.3		
Orthopedic impairments, other health impairments, and multiple disabilities	1.5		
Emotional or behavioral disorder	1.0		
Intellectual disabilities	1.2		

Source: U.S. Department of Education, National Center for Educational Statistics (2008).

How to Use This Information

First, reflect on how your own school looks in relation to national norms. Do the trends in your school echo those across the country? The point of asking these questions is not to label or categorize your students (or to limit your own perceptions of their abilities) but rather to gain a sense of who your students are and what their needs are. What does the diversity of your school population tell you about your students' needs? How might your students' needs differ from those in the general national population? (This fact is important to keep in mind if you are using curricular resources, such as predesigned curriculum materials, designed by a national company rather than your own district or school.)

Second, engage in the same reflection regarding your own students, in your own classroom. Perhaps your students are representative of the school's demographics; perhaps they are a specific subset of the school's population. Either way, it is important to place their needs in context. Again, consider what challenges—and opportunities—are presented by the unique composition of your student population. No other teacher has exactly the same students you do; no other teacher has the same potential to impact those students' lives in the same way.

As classroom demographics change, it is essential for schools to provide up-to-date professional development so that teachers can meet the needs of the students in their classrooms.

Paradoxically, we advocate a cross-categorical approach, yet we believe that at the same time we must be aware of what categories exist and what similarities exist across categories. This is so because many diverse learners are not incidental learners. Strategies must be purposefully chosen with students' particular needs in mind—yet inclusively implemented so that students are not separated from the general education population. For example, the use of visual aids is an excellent strategy to make content accessible to students—but may be inappropriate and ineffective for a visually impaired student. For that student, using a study buddy, auditory cues and repetition, and braille materials are much more effective strategies, all of which can be implemented in the general education setting.

It is important to recognize that these categories can bring additional information about your students, their backgrounds, and their needs—but categories can also be misused. When categories are used to create or validate stereotypes, without reference to individual learners and their needs, they cease to become useful. Similarly, when categories are used to stratify student groups rather than to plan for responsive instruction that looks to similarities across and between categories, they are no longer useful and, in fact, become destructive to student achievement. In the past, categories have been used in society as a means of oppression, which may make some hesitant to use defined groups at all. It is important to recognize the goal in categorical analysis: to become aware of students' needs, beliefs, and backgrounds in order to access resources, instructional strategies, and cultural information that will help them learn.

In any situation, there is always the point where we ask, "What practical benefit will this information have?" How will understanding the diversity of your classroom help you to plan for more effective instruction to meet the academic, linguistic, cultural, and affective needs of students? What information do we need to understand regarding diversity and its impact on teaching?

2. Consider your students' language backgrounds: Is your instruction linguistically accessible?

What does your student population look like, linguistically speaking? Are all of your students fully proficient in English? Do you have a number of ELL students? If so, what level of English language proficiency do they demonstrate? Do you have other students who struggle with language for reasons of disability, culture, or other factors?

Frequently, in thinking about language, special needs, and other issues, we fall into a "deficit" model of thinking, where we consider only the drawbacks or limitations of students' linguistic, cultural, physical, cognitive, and other diversities. In this activity, we suggest you consider not just the linguistic diversity of your students but also some potential benefits or strengths that the students may exhibit. For example, a student who is an ELL but who is fluent in Spanish may be able to translate some materials for other students, may respond well to use of Spanish songs and bilingual books in class, and may have an ability to serve as an interpreter for family members or other parents in the class. A student with an autism spectrum disorder may have challenges in using language to describe events but may have unusually strong sequencing and memory skills—which you can use in scaffolding language activities that will help that student develop descriptive, expressive skills.

Therefore, we ask you to consider students' language proficiencies in the chart (see Figure 1.5), to think about instructional approaches (and accommodations) that may benefit each student, and to list three possible benefits or strengths which you can teach to. While this chart is organized for you to consider one student in your classroom, we encourage you to repeat the process with various students and to share your thoughts and findings with colleagues.

How to Use This Information

In an ideal world, every lesson plan and every teacher will be responsive to the needs of every student, at all times. However, as teachers and teacher trainers ourselves, we are aware that real life interferes. The fire drill fourth period,

Figure 1.5   Impact of Language on Instruction

Consider *three students* in your classroom who appear to demonstrate some type of linguistic diversity. You may consider students with a language-processing disability or an autism spectrum disorder, students with cognitive impairments, or ELL students. Please identify and reflect on the following factors:

Student (Name, or Pseudonym if Chart Will Be Shared)	Language Issues for Student	Benefits and Strengths of Student's Language-Use Patterns	Instructional Strategies That May Benefit Student
		1. 2. 3.	1. 2. 3.
		1. 2. 3.	1. 2. 3.
		1. 2. 3.	1. 2. 3.

the assembly that shortens your testing time, the community events that can interfere with students' abilities to attend and to focus . . . all of these are factors that can undermine the best-laid lesson plans. Therefore, it is important not to take responsiveness for granted, but rather to be deliberate in planning for the needs of students who are not incidental learners. Students who are CLD (culturally and linguistically diverse) and ELLs need deliberate and consistent structure, activities, and plans in order to have the ability to access learning every day, every class. Teachers need opportunities to reflect on their students' needs—and a meaningful way in which to connect the students' needs to instruction.

We suggest you use this chart (Figure 1.5) as a springboard for developing and trying new strategies, approaches, and activities that build on your students' strengths and existing skill sets. Think first of all about your students and what they bring to the table, so to speak. Then, think about the ways in which we view student characteristics. Often, we unconsciously fall into that deficit-model thinking, which blinds us to the abilities and strengths that students do have. Thinking about student "can-ness" (the abilities and talents that do exist rather than those that appear to be missing) can provide a powerful way to reframe both your individual lessons and your overall approach to teaching.

3. Consider your students' experiences: What do they bring to the class?

In structuring our classroom expectations, we frequently forget to think about what students have experienced, what their home and family lives may be like, what beliefs and attitudinal sets they bring with them, and what values they may hold dear and how those values impact their school participation. For this activity, please select one of your students and consider the factors in Figure 1.6.

How to Use This Information

As in the list of academic English words (see Figure 1.2), we frequently forget how the context and background of our students influence their abilities to meet standards and attain objectives. Consider the different areas of impact that you've identified—and that is just for one student! The thought of identifying and differentiating for every student's needs may seem overwhelming at this point. However, the rest of this book is designed to provide you a step-by-step guide to working through the needs of students, ensuring your classroom routines and instructions are responsive to those needs, and collaborating with colleagues to evaluate your progress toward responsiveness on a schoolwide level as well.

Educators are increasingly cognizant that families, and family structures, have become less homogenous and more diverse.

Figure 1.6 Student Background Survey

Question	Answer	Potential Impact on Learning
With whom does the student live?		
What is the student's cultural and linguistic background? (Does the student speak another language or dialect? How proficient in each language is the student?)		
What cultural or religious beliefs does the student have?		
How long has the student's family been in the United States? Have they lived in the same area the entire time?		
What is the student's socioeconomic status?		
How does the student's family perceive school? Perceive school authority and teacher authority?		
Who is the student's peer group?		
What prior educational experiences has the student had?		
What prior social experiences has the student had?		

SUMMARY

As the diversity of the nation, our schools, and our classrooms changes, we recognize the importance of understanding student backgrounds, language proficiencies and skills, and instructional needs. The charts and guides presented in this chapter provide a format for you to think through the issues and reflect on the impact of diversity in your own classroom, for your own students. The impact of diversity can frequently be linked to student language proficiency and the demands of academic English, social and cultural factors, and the background and skills that students bring to the class.

EXTENSION AND COLLABORATION

Take a few minutes to discuss one or more of these questions with a colleague: (You may wish to "partner up" with a coteacher or with someone in your department, grade level, or team and work through these chapters and discussion questions together over the course of the year.)

1. Have the demographics of your school and community changed in the last few years? How? How has this impacted students' abilities to access curriculum?

2. What services and support are available for diverse learners in your school? What additional supports might be useful or helpful to students and teachers?

3. Are there particular issues (background, language, skills) that teachers across the school need to be aware of? Are there concrete steps and strategies that could be provided to all teachers?

4. Consider the students you have in common, if any. What supports or structures could each of you implement in order to build consistent frameworks across classes and services? (Consider students you have simultaneously, such as those who have one teacher for fourth period and another for fifth period. Consider, also, students you may share with another teacher in sequence: if you are a third-grade teacher and your discussion partner is the fourth-grade teacher, for example.)

NEXT STEPS

The next step in this process is to consider how our society has dealt with larger issues of diversity. Being an informed, engaged professional requires one to understand the local and national policy issues—such as welfare reform measures, immigration legislation, and special education law—that impact students' lives. As related to diverse learners, all of the issues discussed in this chapter require a thorough understanding of legal issues impacting diverse learners and of second-language acquisition and acculturation. Therefore, the chapters immediately following this one will deal with those topics, so you can integrate all of these pieces as you consider your classroom instruction, assessment, and interpersonal relationships. As you will consider in Chapter 2, many of these policy and legal issues impact students' abilities to access learning—and many of them are directly linked to student strengths, needs, cultural diversity, language proficiency, and expectations. Before doing so, however, we encourage you to revisit the insights you have gained in this chapter and, even more important, to share them with colleagues: Consider together how you might collaborate to better understand the students within your classrooms and schools. In doing so, you can continue to grow not only as a reflective practitioner but also as a change agent and a leader within your own school, helping others to gain insight into student backgrounds and needs as you have done yourself.

COMMUNITY CONNECTIONS

1. Identify one advocacy group whose work is relevant to your student population—perhaps CEC (the Council for Exceptional Children), a parent organization for students with disabilities, National Council of La Raza (a national Latino advocacy group), or a local advocacy and assistance group. Draft a short summary of the group's work and available resources, and share it with your colleagues at the next staff meeting.

2. Peruse the website of the group you identified and choose one website, link, or resource that would be useful for parents. Send a note home to parents and family members of your students explaining the website and how it might help them. If you have bilingual students, you may wish to ask them to translate the note into their native languages.

3. Select a recent news story from your local newspaper that you feel is relevant to the needs and demographics of your classroom population. Build the news item into a lesson in a manner appropriate for your students' language proficiencies and skills (you may use it in modified form or original form as an introductory motivator, as extended reading, or as a topic for discussion). Post the article on the board of your faculty lounge or copy room so that colleagues can see it (and can see the lesson materials you developed to accompany it!).

USEFUL WEBSITES

- National Clearinghouse for English Language Acquisition: www.ncela .gwu.edu. NCELA provides state and national demographic data.
- Wrightslaw: www.wrightslaw.com/idea/index.htm. Wrightslaw, a legal resource page, offers a wealth of information on the revised Individuals with Disabilities Education Act (2004), covering various topics important to teachers working with students who have exceptionalities.
- Civil Rights Project: www.civilrightsproject.ucla.edu. The UCLA Civil Rights Project (formerly the Harvard Civil Rights Project) is committed to ongoing examination of diversity in our society, and their website has links to a number of research resources, studies, and policy papers on topics including high-stakes testing, special education, and desegregation.

2 The Impact of the Law

Policies and Diversity

Mr. Reyes, the high school principal, sighed as he approached the conference room for his fifth meeting of the day. This particular meeting was one in which his special education department head had specifically asked him to participate. Frequently, the school's substantial number of second-language learner students, and their families, were unintentionally marginalized by the special education referral and identification process, as the maze of procedural safeguards, regulations, and paperwork was enough to confuse even those who had native familiarity with the English language and with the American educational system.

However, today's meeting was different. Catalina, a student who was born in Honduras and who was being evaluated for a potential learning disability, was the student whose case was being discussed. Catalina's older sister, who was pursuing her own undergraduate degree in education, had attended a prior meeting and had fiercely advocated for her sister, challenging what she felt to be the school's inequitable treatment of her sister (she had accused the special educator, in the prior meeting, of "railroading" her sister). As he opened the door to the meeting room, Mr. Reyes found himself regretting the way in which families and school staff often found themselves assuming adversarial roles. As principal, he had been asked to attend in order to support his staff and their handling of the case thus far. Yet he found himself secretly glad that Catalina, unlike many immigrant students, had such a passionate and informed advocate on her side—even if it made his job more difficult.

THE ISSUES

- Mandates for equal protection of students
- Special education law and least restrictive environment
- Assessment and eligibility considerations for CLD (culturally and linguistically diverse) students

- Law and case law on linguistic accessibility of text
- Policy mandates affecting students' daily lives

QUESTIONS TO CONSIDER

1. What laws and regulations are relevant to the school's assessment, placement, and service-delivery process as it is implemented for Catalina?

2. What are the rights of culturally and linguistically diverse students under law?

3. What issues should be addressed in the process of assessment and eligibility determination for special education as it relates to Catalina?

4. In what ways is the school system responsible for making content linguistically accessible for Catalina?

5. How can Catalina's family (and the school) effectively advocate and collaborate for her educational well-being?

GETTING THE ANSWERS

As national and school demographics change, more and more school administrators are being confronted with the dilemmas that faced Mr. Reyes and his staff. These challenges have several components. First, school administrators and teachers may not be aware of relevant policy mandates, particularly for inclusion or assessment of CLD/E (culturally and linguistically diverse exceptional) learners (Collier, 2010). Second, they may feel the school lacks the personnel or resources to appropriately implement policy mandates for inclusive practice, even when they are aware of them (Frattura & Capper, 2006). Third, those educators who are not yet familiar with the impact of second-language acquisition and acculturation may feel themselves to be out of their depth when working with ELL (English language learner) students in the special education process (Artiles, 2003; Baca & Cervantes, 2004; Hoover, Klingner, Baca, & Patton, 2008). Finally, even when educators, families, and advocates do agree on the issues at hand, the complicated nature of the identification process itself may make it difficult to form a productive and collaborative relationship (Harry, 2008).

Legislative mandates drive policy decisions on the district, school, and individual classroom and student levels.

So what does the law say with regard to special education services, accommodations and modifications, and the rights of CLD students? In order to answer this question, it is helpful to look at five core categories of policy and regulations:

1. The legal mandates underlying the special education system and process

2. The legal mandates relating to culturally and linguistically diverse students

3. Accountability requirements for schools and school systems under current law

4. The legal requirements for identification and special education eligibility determination for students who are English language learners

5. Additional related issues (such as immigration policy) and social services available for students and families

The regulations in each of these areas change over time, and they are also too extensive to be summarized in great depth. However, we provide a brief summary of the protections and legal provisions most applicable to ELLs. In the activities that follow, we provide a template for you to self-assess your familiarity with policy mandates and suggest some resources (both within your school system and outside it) for further research.

1. The legal mandates underlying the special education system and process

Special education policy is based on the Individuals with Disabilities Education Act (IDEA), which was most recently updated in 2004 (with final regulations from the Department of Education being posted in 2006). This law guarantees the right of students with disabilities to a free and appropriate public education (FAPE), which is provided through coordination of appropriate services among general educators, special educators, related services personnel (such as speech and language personnel) and other professionals as appropriate. Under IDEA, students are entitled to a timely assessment to determine eligibility for services. Those who qualify are eligible to receive special education services, which are outlined in an individualized family service plan (IFSP) for students from 0 to 3 years of age and in an individualized education plan (IEP) for students from 3 to 21 (or until graduation from high school). The IFSP and IEP should be reviewed annually, at a minimum; should contain goals based on the student's current level of functioning; and are legally binding documents that require consent of the student's parent or guardians (Office of Special Education Programs, 2006). Under federal law, students have a right to be educated in the "least restrictive environment" in which they can be successful, and schools have a corresponding responsibility to prove, if they are removing the student from the general education setting, that the student is not able to succeed in that setting (U.S. Department of Education, 2006).

Under special education legislation, teachers are required to consult with one another and to collaborate in the planning and delivery of services to students with special education needs.

In addition to IDEA, students with disabilities are also covered under Section 504 of the Rehabilitation Act of 1973, which stipulates that any institution receiving federal funding must ensure that individuals with disabilities are not denied "the opportunity to participate in or benefit from" educational or job-related activities, or denied "access to programs, services, benefits, or opportunities." Under this law, students whose disabilities do not qualify them to receive special education services can still receive accommodations under Section 504. This is commonly referred to as a student's "504 plan." Section 504, along with the Americans with Disabilities Act (1990), also protects individuals from job-related discrimination and ensures accessibility for facilities that receive federal funds.

2. The legal mandates relating to culturally and linguistically diverse students

As an English language learner (ELL), Catalina has additional rights under federal legislation and case law. Title III of the No Child Left Behind (NCLB) Act of 2001 governs instruction and services for students who are English language learners. In addition, policy has been established through case law. *Lau v. Nichols* (1974), one of the most famous cases in the history of bilingual education, strengthened the rights of students who are English language learners, as the Supreme Court ruled that school districts were obligated to take necessary steps to provide ELL students with access to the education provided. *Castañeda v. Pickard* (1978) further delineated the rights of CLD students, as the appellate court deciding the case provided three criteria that school districts must follow in selecting programming for CLD students: First, the program must be based on "sound educational theory"; second, it must be implemented with sufficient resources for success; and third, it must be proven effective over time (Hakuta, 2007). While various states have taken diverse positions on the rights of students to bilingual education and native-language support, these criteria still play a role today in shaping the view that educators take of bilingual and ESOL (English for speakers of other languages) programming.

In addition, services for ELL students are governed by Title III of NCLB. The government provides resources for teacher education, professional development, and student services; and at the same time, schools and school systems accepting these funds are held accountable for student performance. These requirements are discussed in the next section.

3. Accountability requirements for schools and school systems under current law

As many educators are all too aware, the meaning and structure of school accountability has changed significantly in recent years. Since the No Child Left Behind Act was passed in 2001, schools and school districts have been held accountable (through the law's Title I) for performance of students as an aggregated group and also for students in various disaggregated subgroups—in other words, for student populations as identified by ethnic group, socioeconomic status, English language proficiency, and status with regard to special education placement. Schools that do not show an acceptable rate of improvement are at first provided additional resources but then are subject to sanctions, which could range from ongoing monitoring by the district to restructuring of the entire school and release of the entire staff. While the federal law has not, to this point, held classroom teachers accountable, the predictable trickle-down effect is that school systems and administrators do put increased pressure on classroom teachers to ensure all students meet achievement standards. Some educators feel this has contributed to a culture of "teaching to the test," while others applaud the fact that the law has at least drawn attention to the achievement of students who have previously often been marginalized in traditional academic settings (National Education Association, 2009).

With regard to special education, the law has been modified slightly from its original parameters. States have been allowed to increase the number of special education students (those with severe and profound disabilities) who are given an alternative assessment because they are unable to access the general education curriculum in any form or with any accommodation or modification. States have the option of administering a modified assessment for these students, which can consist of portfolio assessments or other nonstandardized measures providing some measure of flexibility from the standardized testing requirement (Council for Exceptional Children, 2007).

Less well-known is the structure of accountability under Title III, which governs English language acquisition services. Title III is administered by the Office of English Language Acquisition, Language Enhancement, and Academic Achievement for Limited English Proficient Children (more often known simply as OELA). Under Title III, school systems must also ensure that students who are English language learners make adequate progress toward attaining English language proficiency. If students do not make adequate progress toward English language mastery, school systems and states are subject to sanctions and loss of funding (National Clearinghouse for English Language Acquisition, 2009). Like the provisions in Title I, the Title III provisions have both drawn welcome attention to the achievement of English language learners and contributed to an increased emphasis on standardized means of measurement for language acquisition and proficiency, which can be problematic from the standpoint of linguistic appropriateness, second-language acquisition, and acculturation (Abedi, 2004).

Teacher quality legislation requires teachers to master a content area and to demonstrate skills in pedagogy as well as in areas such as family involvement, teaching diverse learners, and other topics required by each state.

The law's Title II, which deals with teacher quality, has also had an impact on the culture of schools. Under Title II, each teacher must meet strict standards in content area (the law refers to this as being "highly qualified"). Even ESOL and special education teachers are required to demonstrate subject-matter competency in one or more academic areas, under the rationale that they will be working with their specific student populations in order to support those students' acquisition of content, and therefore, they need to have demonstrated proficiency in one or more content areas. States are permitted to set their own criteria for teacher qualification, which typically involves demonstration of coursework in a content area as well as in education theory and methods, a passing test score in the content area, or another means determined appropriate by the state Board of Education to document experience and training (U.S. Department of Education, 2006).

4. The legal requirements for identification and special education eligibility determination for students who are English language learners

As might be expected, this set of laws has placed pressure on school systems to reexamine not only their service-delivery models, curricula, and instructional methods but also the composition of each subgroup on whose performance they are assessed. Some teachers we have met, in fact, complain that their schools are now much more reluctant to qualify ELL students for special education services: Such a decision would identify a student at risk for poor test performance with two subgroups rather than just one, therefore doubling the school's risk of not making adequate yearly process and being sanctioned by the government.

However, such placement decisions must always be made with an eye toward federal mandates. IDEA 2004 contains specific provisions for the assessment process of culturally and linguistically diverse students. These students have a right to be assessed in the language in which they are most likely to be successful and to have procedural paperwork translated into their native language for parents or guardians. States and school systems are required to collect data and review it to ensure that minority or ELL students are not disproportionately placed in special education. In addition, the law stipulates that the decision to qualify a student for special education services (specifically in categories such as that of learning disability, where issues such as language proficiency can sometimes appear to impact the student's performance) cannot be based exclusively or "primarily" on factors such as existing visual, hearing, or motor disability; prior schooling or reading instruction (or lack thereof); emotional disturbance (unless the student is qualified under the category of emotional disturbance); cultural factors; economic or environmental "disadvantage"; or English language proficiency. Schools have a choice, under the 2004 IDEA, between using the more traditional "discrepancy" model to qualify students for special education services or using a newer process called response to intervention (RTI). Under the discrepancy model, students' cognitive (IQ) scores are compared to their academic achievement scores, and if a specific degree of difference (often 15 scaled points) exists between the two assessments, the student is determined to have a learning disability. Under RTI, the emphasis is on providing appropriate intervention at the earliest opportunity, with the first two or three tiers of interventions provided in the general education setting. Under IDEA, school systems may use up to 15% of their special education funds for early intervention services delivered in the general education setting, with the goal of providing support to students before academic difficulties occur, in order to avoid unnecessary or inappropriate placements in special education (Office of Special Education Programs, 2004).

As one might guess, school systems and schools themselves have differing interpretations of the "exclusionary factors" clause with regard to qualification of ELLs for special education. The law does not prohibit ELLs from receiving special education services; it simply seeks to ensure that their placement in special education is due to an actual disability rather than to perceived ethnic, cultural, linguistic, socioeconomic, or emotional differences. However, the law, as is, creates a disincentive for schools to "double-code" students: Schools are potentially accountable for what may be considered inappropriate placement of students in special education, and students' membership in two or more subgroups can increase the difficulty of making adequate yearly progress (AYP) for government reporting purposes (National Education Association, 2009).

5. Additional related issues (such as immigration policy) and social services available for students and families

Frequently, factors such as those mentioned above (socioeconomic, linguistic, cultural, or other differences) have a more significant impact on students' achievement than our current school policies might have us believe. In the spirit of Maslow's (1943) hierarchy of needs, we believe that students' basic needs (for food, shelter, safety, and affirmation) must be met before learning can occur. It would be a challenge for any adult, let alone a young student new to this country, culture, and educational system, to focus for an eight-hour school day while hungry, exhausted from staying up all night with a baby sibling while a parent worked, or fearful of a family member's impending deportation. Yet our culturally and linguistically diverse students all too frequently deal with challenges such as these, or ones even more consuming, which are often "invisible" to school personnel who do not have the opportunity to see the student's home life or prior experiences. We once worked with a high school student who had arrived back in the United States (after a six-year return to his native Mexico) following a 20-day trek through the desert with his father, hiding from immigration officials because his father (unlike him) was not authorized to be in the country. It is no surprise that this student, once he began school, needed time to acclimate to his new setting, to realize he himself was once again safe, and to process his coexisting fears about his father's legal status. His first semester of school in the United States was a challenge socially as well as academically. Yet two years later, the student is successful and is planning to attend community college; exemplifying resiliency, mental wellness, and strength as opposed to the "emotionally disturbed" label that some teachers had suggested, earlier in his career, might be appropriate for him. Indeed, social withdrawal, and so forth, might be an appropriate response for the student in response to those events; and the student's response after such trauma confirms that he was a typically developing student with typical and appropriate reactions—whether those were recognized as such by his teachers or not.

As our school population continues to diversify, teachers must familiarize themselves with the laws and resources available to students such as this one, so that they can appropriately identify students' needs and offer genuine support where possible.

Students are impacted by policy in several areas:

a. *Immigration.* As complicated as our federal laws frequently are, it is our belief that the immigration system is among the most complex (and seemingly arcane) sets of laws in existence, rivaled only by the tax code in its ability to confuse. The United States currently grants legal status to immigrants for several reasons: economic (e.g., a potential immigrant has a needed job skill and is sponsored by an American employer); social (e.g., a potential immigrant has an immediate family member in the United States); moral or humanitarian (e.g., a potential immigrant or refugee demonstrates a risk of harm in their native country and is granted asylum as a result); and for a very limited number of immigrants from select countries, cultural or pluralistic (e.g., a potential immigrant represents a population that is considered to be underrepresented here or would contribute to the diversity of the country) (Batalova, 2006). Of the 39.9 million foreign-born individuals in the United States in 2008, nearly a third have come through "unauthorized" channels and are subsequently considered to be unauthorized or "undocumented" immigrants. An immigrant's undocumented status can impact life in a number of ways, ranging from eligibility for legal employment to eligibility for health care, social services benefits, and, in almost all states, driving privileges (Congressional Budget Office, 2006). An undocumented immigrant may be deported even if he or she has young children here who are authorized immigrants or U.S. citizens themselves. (The children are allowed to remain and may be emancipated, may live with other family members, or may be placed in foster care.) This situation has occurred in increasing numbers in recent years (Barbassa, 2007).

b. *Social Services Such as TANF.* After the welfare reform movement of the 1990s, the federal Temporary Assistance for Needy Families program was developed to replace the centralized federal welfare program previously in existence (U.S. Department of Health and Human Services [USDHHS], 2007). This program provides block grants to states to administer financial assistance programs to families who meet guidelines for being in poverty; therefore, welfare programs may vary from state to state, unlike the national prereform program in existence until the late 1990s (USDHHS, 2007). TANF is designed to support the return of adults to the workforce, so benefits expire after a set period of time if the individual is not attempting to return to work or to obtain an education. TANF assistance is available only to legal immigrants who have been in the United States five or more years (USDHHS, 2007; Batalova, 2006).

c. *Availability of Health Care.* As indicated above, legal status of CLD students and their families can impact the ability to obtain benefits—both healthcare benefits provided through legal employment and state benefits such as Medicaid. In 2009, Congress reauthorized the Children's Health Insurance Program, which helps states extend insurance to children in poverty (Centers for Medicare and Medicaid Services, 2009). In response to the immediacy of health-care issues, and to the evident impact of physical and mental wellness on student achievement, some schools have begun to explore ways to connect families to community health resources to support both well care and sick care (Boethel, 2004). Such projects can play a valuable role in helping students to access learning, as students' ability to succeed in school can often be hindered by family members' illnesses, as well as students' own medical issues.

NEW STEPS TO TAKE—TOMORROW

1. Review your own knowledge of policy mandates and best practices.

As described in the preceding paragraphs, the policy landscape most relevant to CLD/E students includes several different mandates, laws, and bodies of case law: those that impact students with disabilities; those that impact ELLs and culturally diverse students; and those that impact availability of social services, community resources, and school and systemwide supports. Understanding the policy landscape requires educators to have familiarity with each of these in order to identify how to most appropriately serve each student according to the student's linguistic, cultural, cognitive, and academic needs (Herrera & Murry, 2006)—a daunting task for any classroom teacher who is also learning local, school-based, and classroom requirements while also staying current in the content area! This activity asks you to reflect on the areas where you feel most familiar—or least familiar—with different policies and trends, and it suggests some resources to help you gain that familiarity in areas where you might lack it (see Figure 2.1).

Figure 2.1 Policy Landscape: Checking for Understanding

Policy Area or Student Population Served	I understand most policy requirements for this population.		In-School Resources to Support Understanding of Students' Needs	Out-of-School Resources to Learn More
	YES	NO		
Section 504			Civil rights contact for school district special educator or other administrator who oversees Section 504 compliance	• Office of Health and Human Services' Office of Civil Rights • local disability rights groups (parent resource centers, etc.)
IDEA or special education			Special education staff	• Office of Special Education and Rehabilitative Services' (OSER) IDEA (www.ed.gov/idea) • Council for Exceptional Children (www.cec.sped.org) • National Education Association (www.nea.org)
English language learner (ELL) students			ESOL personnel; ESOL, or bilingual, counselor or social worker	• OELA (www.ed.gov/oela) • National Clearinghouse for English Language Acquisition (NCELA) (www.ncela.gwu.edu)
Special education eligibility for ELLs			ESOL personnel, special education staff	• OSERS' IDEA (www.ed.gov/idea) • NCELA (www.ncela.gwu.edu) • National Education Association (www.nea.org) • RTI Action Network (www.rtinetwork.org)
Accountability requirements for special populations (CLD students, minorities, those with disabilities, those in poverty, etc.)			Principal, vice principal, or staff development teacher; ESOL personnel; special education personnel	• No Child Left Behind Act (www.nclb.gov) • National Education Association (www.nea.org/esea) • UCLA Civil Rights Project (www.civilrightsproject.ucla.edu)
Immigration law and policy			Social worker or pupil personnel worker	• United States Customs and Immigration Service (www.uscis.gov) • Pew Research Center (www.pewresearch.org)
Welfare, TANF, and social services			Social worker or pupil personnel worker	• United States Department of Health and Human Services (www.hhs.gov) • Center for Medicare and Medicaid (www.medicaid.com) • Kaiser Family Foundation (www.kff.org)

How to Use This Information

First, allocate some quiet time for yourself to reflect on these issues and to fill out the chart in Figure 2.1. Once you identify any areas where you feel your comfort level with policy issues, or your knowledge of current mandates, is limited, use the suggestions in the right-hand column to deepen your knowledge on each particular issue, working either with resource people within your own building or with resources available online.

Once you have identified your own areas of strength and weakness, consider sharing the chart with a colleague so that they can also identify areas where they feel more (or less) familiar with legal requirements. You may find your areas of strength and weakness are complementary, and you can supplement one another's gaps—or you may find you have the same knowledge sets and the same "holes," and you may decide to work together to address them. The chart can also be completed at a team meeting or department meeting so that multiple staff members have the opportunity to discuss the issues involved.

We believe strongly in the concept of "praxis," insofar as it refers to practical applications of knowledge as opposed to accruing expertise in theory alone (Freire & Macedo, 1987).

> Liberation is a praxis: the action and reflection of men and women upon their world in order to transform it.
>
> —Paolo Freire (1993), *Pedagogy of the Oppressed*

Therefore, the next step, once you identify the areas of depth and the gaps in your own knowledge of policy, is to reflect upon how this knowledge can impact your own practice and then, following reflection, to take action. The activity in Figure 2.2 forms a way in which to do so.

2. Reflect on your own school's compliance with policy mandates *and* best practices.

Many educators are not aware of the ramifications of noncompliance to the mandates of 504 and IDEA. School systems, however, often operate with the assumption that "compliance" within schools can be assumed. We suggest that you complete the checklist (Figure 2.2) to identify your own assessment of your school's degree of compliance and then share the same checklist with others in your school to see if their perceptions match yours.

How to Use This Information

As you reflect on your own school's degree of compliance with policy mandates and best practices (many of which are alluded to in Figure 2.2), consider areas that might be identified for improvement. As part of this process, we strongly suggest you identify two key sets of information:

1. What contributions can *you* make toward closing the knowledge gap? Do you have a good website to share with a colleague on these topics? Or are you

Figure 2.2 School Compliance Reflection Checklist

All teachers are aware of the students with IEPs or 504 plans in their classroom.

_____ Yes   _____ No   _____ Not sure

IEP and 504 plan accommodations are implemented consistently and with fidelity to the written plan.

_____ Yes   _____ No   _____ Not sure

All teachers are aware of the students with ELL plans and are aware of the accommodations recommended for each student.

_____ Yes   _____ No   _____ Not sure

ELL accommodations are implemented consistently and with fidelity to the written plan.

_____ Yes   _____ No   _____ Not sure

A process exists at the school or district level for identifying ELL students who may qualify for special education services.

_____ Yes   _____ No   _____ Not sure

All staff are aware of the relevant policies regarding identification of ELL students who may qualify for special education services.

_____ Yes   _____ No   _____ Not sure

Staff are aware of accountability requirements for CLD/E students.

_____ Yes   _____ No   _____ Not sure

Despite accountability requirements, decisions for placement, instruction, and assessment for students in various subgroups are made with the best interests of the student in mind (rather than with priority given to accountability implications).

_____ Yes   _____ No   _____ Not sure

Staff are aware of the varied resources available for their students and families (including social services, physical and mental wellness care, assistance with basic living, and job-seeking supports).

_____ Yes   _____ No   _____ Not sure

The school has a mechanism to connect students and families with appropriate resources for social services, physical and mental wellness care, assistance with basic living, and job-seeking supports.

_____ Yes   _____ No   _____ Not sure

in a professional role where you have the ability to share information and influence decision making at the school level?

2. Who, within the school, might be a good partner for your efforts to make the school more "CLD/E friendly"? Perhaps an assistant principal, department chair, or even the administrative secretary might be willing to give some time to review the results of the survey with you, to identify areas to address in future staff development, and to provide some opportunities for you or others to directly share information with the staff.

Once you have identified these areas, you can set about the process of being a change agent! This may mean sharing materials with others, or leading a staff development session. It may also mean simply being willing to advocate for your CLD/E students, share information about second-language acquisition in the lunchroom, and watching them "from afar" as they progress to other grades.

3. Discuss relevant policy questions with colleagues.

Often, it is easier to discuss policy issues when discussing a hypothetical situation, where everyone feels free to examine the issues and to express a viewpoint without fear of offending someone directly involved. The set of scenarios in Figure 2.3 provides such an opportunity to do so; it provides two different perspectives on similar issues. These may be useful to discuss in small groups or to share with your entire staff at a faculty meeting. We suggest that, in doing so, you point out that one scenario is written from the administrator's point of view and the other is written from a classroom teacher's vantage point. These may help to tease out some areas of differing assumptions, or even outright disagreements, in your discussions. Keep in mind that any issue, whether at the "policy" level or the "practice" level, looks different when examined from several diverse points of view. Collaboration begins with the recognition that others may have different opinions but also, more than likely, bring additional knowledge and points of view to the table, which must be considered in formulating schoolwide solutions. (Regardless of differences, all participants in a discussion still deserve the presumption of good faith!)

How to Use This Information

These scenarios, as you might guess, will be most valuable if used to facilitate discussion among professionals who bring different sets of expertise and points of view. You may wish to suggest that half the group discuss one scenario and half discuss another, with some time afterward to review each group's ideas and provide whole-group sharing. You may also wish to suggest teachers pair up with partners and review both scenarios in turn. The principal may have a very different perspective on Eduardo's placement from that of the classroom teacher; each operates within a different context and framework. Some principles and practices are indeed nonnegotiable (for example,

Figure 2.3 Parallel Scenarios

Directions: Please read the following brief scenarios. Then take a few minutes to note your response. After the reflection period, please share with your small group. After small-group discussion, we will then share responses as a large group.

Scenario 1

You are the assistant principal of Fairview Middle School in a highly diverse district. The school did not make AYP last year, due to the performance of students in the LEP (limited English proficiency) and special education subgroups, and is being monitored by the central office. Your school currently has 1,000 students, 600 of whom are ELLs. Only 2 of those 600 students are receiving special education services. (Of the non-ELL students, about 40, or 10%, receive special education services. The U.S. Department of Education has indicated that, for proportional representation, approximately 10% to 13% of any given population can be assumed to have special education needs.) Your principal has asked you to develop a plan to ensure appropriate identification, coding, and service delivery for English language learners in the school who may also have special needs. You accept the assignment, knowing that students coded in two subgroups are often seen as "double jeopardy" students and that, for purposes of AYP, having students dually coded may make it more difficult to achieve satisfactory progress in the LEP and special education subgroup, because one student's score may count several times. In recent years, there seems to be an increased focus throughout the district on minimizing representation of ELLs in the special education subgroup.

What would be your first step in attempting this task? Would you advocate for additional inclusive assessment procedures that might increase the number of dually coded students? Would you advocate for a process that would maintain the current ratio of representation, though it may seem disproportionate? What issues are at stake, and how would you prioritize those issues?

Scenario 2

You are a classroom teacher, teaching reading to seventh-grade students at Fairview Middle School, located in a highly diverse district. The school did not make AYP last year, due to the performance of students in the LEP and special education subgroups, and is being monitored by the central office. Your school currently has 1,000 students, 600 of whom are ELLs. Only 2 of those 600 students are receiving special education services. (Of the non-ELL students, about 40, or 10%, receive special education services.) You are becoming increasingly concerned about Eduardo, one student in your class. Eduardo is a Level 3 (on the LAS Links English proficiency scale) ESOL student who participates in some ESOL classes as well as general education, nonsheltered courses. Eduardo arrived in the United States five years ago and currently lives with his mother and two younger brothers. You have concerns because, even if he is speaking or writing in his native language with friends, Eduardo appears to process information at a slower rate than his peers, appears to have difficulty putting thoughts down on paper, and becomes easily frustrated and discouraged. These issues are also of concern in your class, where Eduardo struggles to complete reading and writing assignments even when he receives ESOL accommodations. While you are not trained in special education, you are concerned about the possibility of a learning disability that may be interfering with Eduardo's ability to make progress in his classes or to acquire standard English proficiency. You speak to the special education department chair, who agrees to begin a prereferral process but indicates it is highly unlikely that Eduardo would be placed in special education, due to his status as an ELL.

How would you respond to this individual? Based on the department chair's feedback, what reactions would you have about placement and service delivery for Eduardo? What interventions, if any, might help Eduardo to be successful in your class? What interventions or support, schoolwide, might help Eduardo to succeed in his other classes too?

placement should not be based on culturally biased assessments; students should not be placed in special education based simply on language proficiency or prior schooling). At the same time, the question of how each school community must implement policy mandates is one that deserves input from every member of the school community, in a process that respects opinions, perspectives, and unique expertise.

Consider using role play to structure your discussion of these two scenarios. Among other things, one goal of this exercise is for participants to realize that the same issue may look very different from the classroom teacher's perspective as opposed to the administrator's—and to begin to identify ways to bridge the gap between the two perspectives.

SUMMARY

While policy issues may seem to be removed from the day-to-day events of classroom instruction, they are, in reality, anything but removed. Policy mandates have an ongoing impact on the demographics of our student population (through regulation of immigration and availability of support), the placement of students (through special education, ESOL, and assessment requirements), standards-based instruction and assessment (through NCLB and also through IDEA), and the process that we use to provide support to struggling students (through both NCLB and IDEA). For that reason, teachers must not only be aware of what the law requires but must also take time to think through the value of collaboration, in order to learn from each others' areas of expertise so that students in all subgroups can be successful in the most appropriate setting, with appropriate curriculum, instruction, and assessment.

EXTENSION AND COLLABORATION

Understanding the "policy process" and the nature of policy requires that teachers not only have a basic knowledge of legal mandates (nationally; at the SEA—state education agency—level; at the LEA—local education agency—level; and within their own school system), but that educators also think critically about the role of teachers as advocate, using their knowledge of policies to identify ways to improve the educational process for their students.

In this section, we encourage you to identify ways that you might deepen your own knowledge of policy—and also share that knowledge with colleagues, family members, and students:

1. Suggest to your administrators that a representative from a local advocacy group visit your staff meeting to share some information about what their organization does and what needs they serve.

2. Involve your students in the process of thinking about policies that impact them . . . from immigration law, to welfare reform, to equal protection

laws (discussion of Title IX and gender equity is often sure to spark discussion in a middle or high school classroom). You may wish to have students discuss a particular law or policy, then create materials in English and in their native languages, so they can take them home and share with their family members, too.

3. Suggest that your administrators or staff developers focus on a "policy of the month," with 5 to 10 minutes of discussion at department and staff meetings each month dedicated to sharing information about a particular policy impacting student achievement. For example, your special educators (or other appropriate personnel) could spend five minutes reviewing provisions of Section 504 one month; the school's pupil personnel worker, social worker, or counselor could spend a brief amount of time reviewing social services policies and supports; or the ESOL personnel could provide a brief overview of ESOL testing and placement, so all staff members have access to the same foundational information.

NEXT STEPS

After considering the spectrum of legal mandates that impact the presence and success of CLD/E students in the classroom, the next step is to consider how, specifically, the classroom setting accommodates their needs. Doing so requires an awareness not just of the legal and social context for diverse learners' success but also of the myriad of other factors that impact student growth and achievement. One of these, frequently overlooked, is classroom setup. In consistency with Maslow's (1943) principles, and with theories of constructivist learning (Crotty, 1998), diverse learners are best served when the physical space is one that meets their needs. In addition, the classroom setting should convey that the student is the most important element in the classroom—all other elements in the classroom (physical and otherwise) are planned and geared toward student success. The following chapter provides some suggestions for creating such an environment in your classroom.

COMMUNITY CONNECTIONS

1. Invite representatives from local advocacy organizations to send you information, or visit during parent nights, so families can receive materials and information about services that may be provided. Legal defense agencies, social service agencies, and special education advocacy groups may be a powerful source of information for parents and family members who are trying to navigate the system on their own.

2. Check with your local teachers' association or union to identify upcoming bills and current issues. It may be possible to facilitate change with a minimum of effort—you could circulate a petition to be signed (within the parameters of your school policies, of course), speak briefly to colleagues at a staff meeting, or post information in the staff lounge.

3. Consider hosting a family or community forum dedicated to educating family members about policy issues. Topics might include the school's testing and assessment policy, placement and educational issues for English language learners, and school performance and accountability. One school with which we are familiar decided to host a parent forum on the topic of diversity, with the goal of empowering parents to identify ways in which the school could better serve culturally and linguistically diverse learners. You may find that local organizations (or even your school district's ESOL office) would be willing to help sponsor the event, contribute facilitators or speakers, or provide refreshments or other materials.

USEFUL WEBSITES

Some of the best resources for policy and research are highlighted in the self-assessment table provided earlier in this chapter (see Figure 2.1). The full citations and descriptions are given here for some of the most frequently used websites; consult the table for additional ones:

- National Clearinghouse for English Language Acquisition (NCELA): www.ncela.gwu.edu. NCELA provides a comprehensive set of resources on language proficiency, academic standards for ELLs, assessment and instruction, and relevant legal and policy issues.
- Council for Exceptional Children: www.cec.sped.org. The CEC website contains information on rights of students with disabilities, special education law and policy (with particular attention to IDEA 2004), and current research on topics related to special education.
- Pew Research Center: www.pewresearch.org, and Pew Hispanic Center: www.pewhispanic.org. The Pew Research Center and its related center, the Pew Hispanic Center, collect and disseminate a variety of resources on topics related to numerous policy issues. In particular, the Centers' information on demographics and immigration policy is comprehensive and frequently updated.
- National Education Association: www.nea.org. The NEA website likewise contains information about numerous policy issues, including accountability, special education, and RTI implementation.
- RTI Action Network: www.rtinetwork.org. The RTI Action Network aims to provide information to teachers and other practitioners interested in RTI and to provide a means for them to connect with one another. The Network operates a comprehensive website and maintains a presence on social networking sites such as Facebook to facilitate easy and timely communication with members.

3 What a Difference a Room Makes

Classroom Setup and Management for Learning

Elena Murphy, a third-grade teacher in an inclusive and linguistically diverse classroom, thought she had done everything right to get her year off to a great start: She had sent lengthy notes home to parents detailing her expectations, posted her eight classroom rules at the front of the room on brightly colored sentence strips, and reviewed the rules on the first day and clearly spelled out the consequences for misbehavior. She had even tagged various objects around the room with English and Spanish words, in an attempt to be responsive to the needs of the English language learners in her class of 24. As she had six students with individualized education plans (IEPs) (for perceptual and physical disabilities, learning differences, and a behavioral disorder) and a seventh who had a 504 plan in place for a hearing impairment, she consulted regularly with the special education teachers and paraprofessionals. Yet she couldn't seem to get any of her students to attend to the task at hand, to follow directions, or even to go to the right centers for activity time. In frustration, she finally went to a more experienced colleague and asked for help. She was surprised at the response she got.

"Have you sat down in one of the desks and looked around the room?" said her colleague. "What do you see when you do that?"

Elena was dubious ("I don't have enough planning time as it is! Why should I spend it sitting in a student's desk?"), but desperate enough to try anything, she went back to her classroom. She thought a moment and then chose the desk where her least attentive student sat, in the fourth row, fifth seat back. What she saw surprised her.

From that seat, sitting down and looking around from the student's level, Elena realized she couldn't see the beautifully lettered classroom rules—they were too far

34

away, too small, and partially obscured by the high-backed chair near the teacher's desk. She realized, too, that it was almost impossible to find where one center began and another ended: The five centers were all lined up along the left side of the room, and they, too, had the same lettering on their labels and no pictures to distinguish them. She thought back to the day before, when she had scolded a student with a visual-processing issue for "wandering" around the room, and wondered just how much of her "room" he saw—or how accessible she had made the room.

The Spanish words on which she had worked so hard were not at all at a student's eye level—rather, they were at her own eye level, five feet off the ground. For her student in a wheelchair, they would never be visible. The air conditioning and heating unit behind her made a constant distracting hum in her ear—though, despite the loud noises, it didn't seem to be working all that well, since this corner of the room was uncomfortably hot. The smell of hot dogs wafting in from the school cafeteria one floor below didn't help much either. On all sides, the other students' desks crowded her in, making her feel almost claustrophobic as they were all less than fifteen inches away. Elena realized suddenly that if she, who had no special education needs, had trouble paying attention in this room, it must be unspeakably difficult for her students with IEPs—and for those without IEPs as well! Elena closed her eyes and thought about the way her school day progressed: Students were expected to come in, get their materials for the day from a bin, sharpen pencils before the bell rang, and be quietly working when school began. Opening her eyes, Elena looked for the bin where worksheets and other materials were stored. It was far back on a cluttered shelf—no wonder her students had difficulty finding it and getting materials in a timely manner! From this seat in the room, she had to crane her neck to find the spot on the board (among the six other announcements) where she would post her daily assignments. It crossed her mind, suddenly, that even more than random words in the classroom, it would probably have been helpful to translate some of those assignments' directions into Spanish.

She went back to her colleague's room and flopped down on the comfortable couch that sat at an angle next to the desk in the back of the room. "OK, I understand," she said. "Now I just have to fix it."

THE ISSUES

- Importance of classroom arrangement for learning
- Equitable practices for grouping and seating
- Sensitivity to diverse learning styles
- Sensory needs of students and impact on learning
- Cultural, cognitive, and linguistic issues in planning

QUESTIONS TO CONSIDER

1. How did Elena's perceptions change once she viewed her classroom from a student's perspective?

Classrooms should include a variety of spaces to support developmentally appropriate teaching and learning.

2. What elements in her classroom seemed, at first, to be conducive to learning? What did she realize about those elements when she looked at them from the student's point of view?

3. What features of Elena's classroom setup and physical arrangement might be distracting to students with exceptionalities or culturally and linguistically diverse learners?

4. What should Elena consider as she redesigns and reevaluates her classroom arrangement and procedures?

5. What does Elena's classroom space communicate to her students in terms of academic and behavioral expectations?

6. Whose input might Elena seek in the process of reevaluating and redesigning her classroom arrangement?

GETTING THE ANSWERS

As inclusive models become more of a reality in our schools, general educators, special educators, ESOL (English for speakers of other languages) teachers, and other professionals alike are faced with the task of ensuring that their classrooms are arranged, materials are available, and procedures are structured in such a way as to ensure that all students can access the curriculum. This begins with an overview of every aspect of instruction—starting with the most basic aspects such as classroom setup, management, and procedures.

We frequently think of classroom management as having to do primarily with rules and routines. In this chapter, we suggest, rather, that classroom management begins at the physical, environmental, and interpersonal levels—with careful planning to ensure students are placed in an environment conducive to learning. Placement of desks, accessibility of classroom materials, and the feeling of a welcoming climate are important prerequisites for learning.

Research has overwhelmingly demonstrated the value of activities that "build equitable classrooms" (Lotan, 2006), especially when educators collaborate with one another to do so (Sadker & Sadker, 1988; Klingner et al., 2005). In considering how to arrange your classroom for equitable participation and learning of all students, it is important to be mindful of the other physical factors around your classroom: sources of noise, temperature variations, areas where vision is partially or fully blocked, proximity to others' desks, and proximity to materials. For diverse learners, it is essential to have these issues addressed before learning can occur.

It is also important to consider what your classroom space communicates to students. Does the classroom indicate that it is time for play? Serious work? (How does one distinguish between the two?) Are we telling students not to look at one another's work, or not to work together, when the arrangement of desks makes it difficult for them to comply with our directions? Figure 3.1 provides further information about how classroom setup is important for students with varying needs.

As important as classroom setup is the issue of equitable practice. Research also indicates the importance of structuring classroom rules and procedures in an equitable way that ensures equal access and participation for all students. This concept extends to teacher practices (are you calling on all students equally? Providing wait time to all students? Balancing "teacher talk" with "student talk"?) (Kohl, 2002) and also to classroom arrangement (have you

| Figure 3.1 | Impact of Classroom Setup |

An effective classroom arrangement is helpful for all students. For ELL students and students with exceptionalities, though, it is absolutely essential. The following table lists some of the students for whom classroom setup may be a crucial factor in their ability to access learning. This is a representative, not an all-inclusive, list. Again, we believe that while teachers must be aware of the needs that particular students may bring to the classroom, it is essential to see each student as an individual and not to restrict our conceptions of needs based on a label.

- Students with attention difficulties (proximity to others; visibility of materials; and/or desk placement)
- Students with learning differences (visibility of board and instructional materials; proximity to others; and/or accessibility of teacher or paraprofessional support)
- Students with autism spectrum disorders (proximity to others; grouping arrangements; visibility of materials; proximity to teacher; and/or availability of materials and organizational schema)
- Students with hearing impairments (proximity to teacher; grouping arrangements; position in class and proximity to other sources of noise; and/or lighting and visual access for lipreading or signing)
- Students with vision impairments (proximity to teacher; proximity to front of room and blackboard or whiteboard; proximity to materials; and/or grouping arrangements)
- Students with physical challenges (proximity to teacher; grouping arrangements; and/or ease of accessibility to materials, desk, and peers)
- Students with emotional and/or behavioral challenges (grouping arrangements; position in class; proximity to sources of noise and distraction; proximity to peers; and/or proximity to teacher)
- Students who are English language learners (proximity to materials; visibility of materials and board; ease of access to teacher; and/or grouping arrangements)

Space for small-group work, and ready availability of manipulatives, can support learning for all students.

unconsciously placed all your minority or majority students in a particular part of the room? Have you made sure to place students with disabilities near those who do not have disabilities? Do students have needed proximity to materials, teachers, and accessible seating arrangements? How does your classroom setup communicate your behavioral and academic expectations to students?).

Whether working with students who have exceptionalities, students who are English language learners, or both, it is essential for teachers to be aware of their own preconceptions and biases so that they can consider how students' perceptions and abilities may differ from their own. Such awareness is known as "cultural responsiveness" or "cultural competency" (Mason, 1993). Researchers have suggested that cultural competency has several distinct stages: knowledge of one's own cultural identity; awareness and familiarity with other groups, their traditions, and norms; and transformative behavior change (Hanley, 1999, as cited in Hoover, Klingner, Baca, & Patton, 2008).

This framework, focused on knowledge of oneself, knowledge of one's students, and the resolution to change one's practice (Hanley, 1999), provides a way to begin the process of evaluating one's instructional beliefs and activities, starting in this chapter with the most basic elements: the arrangement and accessibility of the learning environment. In this process, it is essential to have an awareness of students' needs and a willingness to adapt one's own expectations rather than to consider them as nonnegotiable "universals." For example, it is legitimate to expect that all students will learn in class. However, it is not legitimate, or universal, to expect all students to sit still while reading, to raise their hands at all times before speaking, or to work cooperatively with any partners assigned to them. For students with varying cultural, cognitive, intellectual, emotional, and physical needs, any or all of these expectations may be unreasonable and impossible to achieve without specific, differentiated support.

To address these issues, we suggest that you first reevaluate the elements of your classroom that may make it difficult for diverse learners (including those who are second-language learners, those who are new to this country or culture, and those who have differing abilities) to access or participate in your instructional activities; and second, develop a systematic plan for addressing any elements that may limit students' ability to access or participate in the curriculum. The list of key items and issues in Figure 3.2 may give you some idea of commonly existing barriers. This is not meant to be an all-inclusive laundry list but, rather, a guide to help you begin looking around your room, and looking at your procedures, with a critical eye.

In thinking about these elements of your classroom, it is key to consider the impact of expectations on students from different cultural backgrounds, as well as those with exceptionalities. A simply stated expectation, such as "Raise your hand to talk," may be problematic for a student with no prior schooling experience, who cannot intuitively make the connection between raising one's hand and being allowed to speak. It may be equally difficult for a student with motor-coordination challenges or impulse-control and attention issues—and careful planning will acknowledge those challenges before the rule is implemented, so alternative procedures can be developed for those students.

Figure 3.2   Variables Contributing to Classroom Accessibility

How big (or small) is the room? What is the temperature? Does the temperature vary throughout the day or year?

Does the furniture "fit" all children and allow students room to move and work?

How is the lighting? Is there a glare? Is the lighting harsh or soft?

Is the room cluttered? Are materials organized in an accessible, easy-to-locate fashion?

How close together are the desks? Are the desks close to materials?

Must students ask for materials, or are materials made accessible so that students can reach them without disrupting others? Can students visually identify where materials are to be found?

What type of work areas do students have? Are work areas differentiated for different student tasks?

Are there "hidden or seductive hazards" (computer space, paint areas, open puzzle areas, open chalk or marker and whiteboard space) that draw students toward them and that may prove to be distracting? If so, how is that distraction factor addressed?

What rules and procedures are posted? Are procedures made accessible to CLD (culturally and linguistically diverse) students? To students with different abilities?

Are written directions posted around the room for students' reference during transitions?

What type of information is communicated to and about students? Is student work posted prominently? Do displays include work that is still in progress, or work that has not met all objectives but represents growth toward the objective?

NEW STEPS TO TAKE—TOMORROW

1. Diagram and review your room arrangement and setup.

Take a blank sheet of paper (or even a sheet of graph paper) and sketch out your classroom, including space for students' desks, teacher workspace, centers, materials, entrances, and exits. Review the list of hidden hazards provided in Figure 3.2 to identify areas that may make it difficult for students to learn. You may wish to sketch out student desks in one color, instructional space and materials in a second color, and hazards or areas of distraction in a third color so you can see the interplay among all three.

How to Use This Information

Typically, every teacher reviews and revises the seating plan at least once a year, whether at the beginning of the year, at the midyear break, or in the middle of a term as a way to keep things interesting for students. However, each time desks and seating arrangements change, students' comfort zones and routines change as well. Sketching the entire classroom—as well as the desks—helps in ensuring that students really are placed appropriately in the physical environment that will help them learn best.

We suggest being creative in how you use this diagram, once you sketch it. You might distribute a partially filled diagram to students and ask them to specify which spaces in the classroom they find least distracting (or most distracting); you might ask students to come up with different desk arrangements and justify their choices. You might distribute the seating chart to family members at a back-to-school night and ask them where they would expect to see their child seated—and why. You might bring your chart to a faculty meeting and share it with colleagues—or ask them for suggestions about particularly challenging spatial issues ("It's so hot by the

Teachers may find it useful to reconfigure desks for activities such as pair-share and partner work.

radiator; no one can concentrate when I put them there. But there are so many desks, I have no choice but to put at least three students next to it. Any ideas?")

2. Survey your students.

To get a sense for what your students need and how they learn best, consider observation (which we will discuss in Chapter 4) and direct questioning. The survey in Figure 3.3 is one way to ask students questions to get information about their learning habits, styles, perceptions of the classroom, and other information needed to plan for instruction. We suggest that you provide these questions to your students—but be creative. Especially when you are trying to assess the learning styles and needs of differently abled students, consider giving the survey in a non-traditional manner. Students could pair up and draw their answers; students could talk about the answers to each other and then share with the class; students could dictate answers to their teacher (you!) or a paraprofessional; students could speak into a tape or digital recorder at a center station. If a student lacks the linguistic skill to answer questions in English, consider asking a more proficient student to translate, or consider observing the student for a specified period of time in order to gather some of this information. (But be careful that you are accurately observing and describing what you see in behavioral terms—as we will discuss further in Chapter 4—rather than simply charting your biases and perceptions.)

How to Use This Information

You may have seen surveys like Figure 3.3 in other books—perhaps your district even has a similar one that it recommends. We believe the questions on this survey are important, as you want to gather students' perceptions on how they learn and on what they need to learn. At the same time, though, no one instrument meets the needs of every student or population. Please feel free to add more material, or exchange questions, if you believe you can come up with questions that address the specific needs of your population. As discussed above, please also modify the survey administration to fit the needs of your students. Perhaps you want to have them fill it out in groups; perhaps you want to ask the questions orally and discuss them as a class; perhaps your students have the literacy and metacognitive skills to fill it out independently. There is no one "right" way to administer this. In fact, if your students are too young or are not able to fully respond to the questions, you may observe students and fill it out based on the results of your observations (but be careful to respond to what you see, rather than what you feel, think, or infer).

After giving the survey to students—in whatever form—we encourage you to consider the results. You may want to line up each survey, one at a time, next to the classroom diagram you created in the preceding activity and consider how students' answers "map" onto the diagram of what already exists in your classroom—or what might exist.

3. Observe and reflect with a colleague.

Ask a peer to spend some time (at least a half hour) in your classroom and to record impressions regarding the accessibility of your classroom, materials, procedures, and arrangements. You may wish to reciprocate and do the same for your colleague (see Figure 3.4).

Figure 3.3   Student Learning Patterns Survey

1. Where do you learn best?

   ____Front of the room   ____Back of the room   ____Middle of the room

   Why?

2. I learn best when (check all that apply)

   ____The room is quiet

   ____The room is noisy

   ____I am listening to music

   ____I have something to hold

   ____I am moving

3. I learn something best by

   ____Watching someone do it

   ____Listening to someone talk about it

   ____Drawing a picture about it

   ____Reading a story about it

   ____Talking about it

   ____Writing about it

   ____Thinking about how it's important in my life

4. I like to work with other people.

   ____Always   ____Sometimes   ____Never

   What kind of work do you like to do with partners or groups?

   What kind of work do you like to do by yourself?

5. When I am doing work, I like to

   ____Sit at my desk   ____Lie on the floor   ____Sit in a comfortable chair or couch   ____Stand up

   Why?

6. I can find all the materials I need to do my work.

   ____Always   ____Sometimes   ____ Never

   Why?

Figure 3.4 Peer Observation Form

Class:
Date:
Period or time of day:
Observer:

Question	Y	N	Not Sure	What do you observe?
1. Look at the desk arrangement. Can all students see the teacher?				
2. Sit in a few different spots of the room. Can you hear clearly at all points? Are there auditory distractions at any point or location?				
3. Look around the room. What visual stimuli might be distracting?				
4. What tactile or sensory stimuli might be distracting? What might students want to touch? Are there smells in the room?				
5. Is board work clearly visible for all students?				
6. Are directions and procedures posted clearly on the board?				
7. Do all students appear to get along with those around them?				
8. Does desk grouping facilitate collaboration? Are students able to work with multiple partners or groups?				

How to Use This Information

As we suggested earlier, we believe the most powerful way to use peer observation is in a collaborative effort, where you and a partner observe one another, offer feedback to one another, and share your opinions and views together to gain from various perspectives. Consider working with a colleague to observe one another's classroom procedures, record your observations, and then reflect together on what you have seen. Collaboration and discussion can provide a valuable way to gain more insight into your own practice by drawing on others' experiences and knowledge.

I not only use all of the brains I have, but all I can borrow.

—*Woodrow Wilson*

4. Take the opposite perspective.

Sometimes, it is helpful to look at our rules and procedures from the perspective of a student who might find them most challenging. Even for experienced and effective teachers, this process of reexamination may be a helpful way to facilitate reflective practice. We suggest listing your classroom procedures on the left side of the chart in Figure 3.5, then breaking down the demands each one makes upon students. For example, a rule such as "Line up and walk to lunch" requires that students have cultural awareness (the awareness of what a line is, why it is important to line up, and where the lunchroom is) as well as motor skills (the ability to move to the line and take one's place in line) and the attentional and behavioral skill needed to follow the direction each day.

Once you have identified the demands that your procedures and expectations place upon students, consider them from the perspective of the student who is most challenged by those expectations and who may exhibit the most difficulty in meeting them. You might wish to brainstorm with colleagues to design scaffolds that might help students adhere to those procedures. Some of the solutions and scaffolds outlined here (or that you come up with) may sound like elements of a behavioral intervention plan (BIP); however, they are offered with the goal of making formal BIPs unnecessary or of making them most effective by allowing teachers to focus on the interventions that have been determined to obtain results.

How to Use This Information

We suggest you fill out the table in Figure 3.5 for each classroom procedure, thinking reflectively and intensively about why students might find the procedure unfamiliar or challenging. As American teachers, we may have taken the framework and core concepts of American school for granted: Of course students know how to raise their hands, sit quietly till called on, line up at lunchtime, and so on. We forget that these are not universal at all but, rather, are part of a culturally dependent framework that diverse learners may, and often do, find unfamiliar at best, problematic at worst.

Figure 3.5	Classroom Procedures and Demands

Classroom Procedure	Demands and Requirements for Students	What student might find this most challenging?	How might we scaffold success?
Raise your hand to speak.	• Appropriate pragmatic/linguistic skill • Appropriate gross motor control • Impulse control • Ability to sustain attention • Familiarity with school procedures/processes	• Students with speech/language challenges • Students with gross motor challenges • Students with attention/behavioral challenges • Students unfamiliar with U.S. school routines	• Provide alternatives (raise a cue card). • Provide an immediate outlet (write the question down on a card and hand it to the teacher). • Provide reinforcement and incentive for following the rule. • Take time to explain the rule; provide a peer buddy or partner for the student.

Use the blank table to fill in and reflect on your own classroom procedures:

Classroom Procedure	Demands and Requirements for Students	What student might find this most challenging?	How might we scaffold success?

SUMMARY

In thinking about inclusive practice, we often overlook some of the most basic elements: classroom setup, arrangement, and familiarity with students' learning needs. In this chapter, we've attempted to provide an overview of why that information is important, as well as to indicate some initial steps to address those issues. The process of looking at your classroom with a critical eye, conscious of the needs of diverse learners, is an important first step in ensuring that you have a solid foundation on which to build your instructional practice. Classroom arrangement, grouping, seating, procedures, and expectations are all part of that foundation. The charts and tools included in this chapter provide a framework for systematically examining those elements and identifying aspects to highlight, modify, or improve.

EXTENSION AND COLLABORATION

As in the first chapter, we provide this information in the hopes that you will use it not only in your classroom but also in your interactions with colleagues. Some suggestions for doing so are provided:

1. Consider sharing your classroom diagram at a staff, team, or department meeting. Share any new ideas you may have—or share the challenges and problems you are still working on. Either way, you may be surprised by the feedback and suggestions you receive from colleagues.

2. Partner with a colleague to do peer observations; or interview one another's students about learning styles, needs, and what works for them. Share the information with your colleague over coffee, in a relaxed conference.

3. Schedule a meeting with your special education team leader or coteacher to review classroom procedures and expectations. If your classroom population is highly diverse, you may wish to invite your ESOL teacher as well. Discuss each procedure or rule that you have in your classroom, and brainstorm ways to make the rules more accessible or easy to accomplish for students with diverse learning challenges.

NEXT STEPS

The next step in this process is to think about the impact of the issues you identified, and the changes you made, in your classroom. Classroom environment cannot be separated from instruction, or from interpersonal dynamics—and future chapters in the book are devoted to examining those topics. After gaining a strong understanding of your expectations for diverse learners—as well as the way in which your classroom allows those students to build on their strengths—the immediate next step in the process is to continue reflective examination of your teaching practices, considering the way in which we typically observe students and make judgments about their abilities. Evaluating your observational and informal assessment practices provides a basis for the activities that occur later in the book, related to assessment, mental health, and modification of instruction.

COMMUNITY CONNECTIONS

1. Classroom expectations and procedures can often be challenging for diverse learners, and communication with students' families is an important part of helping students to succeed in learning those expectations. Consider working with your school team to schedule a workshop for parents, where school expectations are explained (perhaps with interpreters to assist) and parents are asked to give input about their students' prior experiences and areas of success.

2. Often, local businesses may be willing to contribute materials for classrooms. Work with a colleague to create a list of classroom materials that would be useful for diverse learners. This may include school supplies for students who cannot afford to purchase them, large cushions for an independent reading space; or new tables for more clearly defined literacy centers. Create a short description of what you need, and circulate it to local stores and merchants, asking them to contribute in kind. If you do receive contributions, be sure to involve your students in writing thank-you notes and making classroom signs to acknowledge the donors.

3. Consider inviting members of advocacy and cultural awareness groups to present at a staff or team meeting so that they can share information about the background, values, and beliefs that various student groups bring to the classroom. You may wish to ask your administrator to provide some small-group reflection time afterward to brainstorm ways that the school community can act on the information presented.

USEFUL WEBSITES

- The Center for Research on Education, Diversity, and Excellence: http://crede.berkeley.edu. CREDE is devoted to examining issues of pedagogy, equity, and diversity in education, particularly with respect to ELL students. The center also produces a number of CD-ROM case studies appropriate for study and reflection.
- The National Center for Culturally Responsive Educational Systems: www.nccrest.org. NCCREST is a federally funded technical assistance center that provides information and resources to states, organizations, and school systems, as well as makes information available online to individuals. NCCREST provides extensive research and data on culturally responsive educational practices and trends across the nation and by state, along with a section listing specific recommendations and strategies for teachers of diverse populations.
- National Center for Cultural Competence at Georgetown University: www11.georgetown.edu/research/gucchd/nccc. Geared toward mental health professionals, this website provides self-assessment rubrics for determining one's own cultural competence, as well as guides for communicating with others of various cultures.

4 Really Seeing Your Students

The Importance of Behavioral Observation

As Roberto looked out over his class as the bell rang to start the school day, his eyes drifted toward the back of the room. Oliver, a student who had a 504 plan in place for a mild learning disability, sat there and observed the same routine each day. He came in five minutes early, slept with his head on his desk until the bell rang, looked around, and put his head back down.

"He must be really tired today," thought Roberto. As he looked at Oliver, he was reminded of the experience he had when three members of his school's multidisciplinary team came in at three separate times, to observe him for an eligibility determination hearing.

The first teacher had watched Oliver's routine and said to Roberto, "This student is clearly disengaged. Why is he so resistant to your instruction?"

The second teacher had observed Oliver's routine and commented, "I wonder if he has some problems in his home life. If he is not sleeping well, or if he is stressed over something at home, that could be the reason he is depressed or disengaged."

The third team member had looked at Oliver and said, "I just see a student sleeping. The question is, 'What's making him sleep?'"

THE ISSUES

- Importance of accurate observation
- Teachers' perceptions of students' behavior and responses
- Understanding cultural, family, and behavioral norms
- Accurate reporting and drawing of conclusions

QUESTIONS TO CONSIDER

1. How did each team member preconceive what they "saw" in Oliver?

2. How did each team member's perspective on Oliver's needs impact what they might recommend as an intervention?

3. How would you describe Oliver's behavior in class? List the reasons that underlie it.

4. Why is it important for Oliver's teachers to accurately describe his behavior and to state his actions and needs in behavioral terms?

GETTING THE ANSWERS

You may be familiar with the phrase, popularized by the performer Flip Wilson in the 1970s, that "what you see is what you get." When it comes to school-related issues, we believe that what one sees is, in fact, influenced largely by what we are willing and available to see. In other words, our preconceptions, biases (those we acknowledge and those we may not even be aware of), and our prior experience may limit how we "see" a given situation and, therefore, limit what our response may be. This is apparent by looking at another example, similar to the one described above but based in real experience. One of us was invited to attend an eligibility determination meeting for a student we knew, whose parents had requested a meeting regarding special education services because the student's grades were steadily declining. The student was eight years old, and his teachers reported at the meetings that he was "unmotivated," "disrespectful," and "resistant" to their efforts to provide instruction. When asked to clarify and explain what, in particular, the student did, the teachers replied: "He refuses to put his head up." "He won't listen to what I say." "His behavior is very erratic. He sleeps in fits and starts during class, and then wakes up. But he is always in a bad mood when he wakes up, and he won't do what I say." At this point in the meeting, the student's mother shared that the student had been taking medication, for the past six months, which had well-documented side effects of drowsiness and irritability. The student's doctor was beginning to wean him off the medication, a process that was expected to take another two months. We recommended that the teachers and parents agree on a plan to ensure the student did not miss class content while the transition period was continuing, and reevaluate for special education services if the student continued to have difficulty even with that plan in place.

Imagine how much sooner the student could have received support if the chain of events had gone this way:

> The classroom teacher notices the student is sleeping in class. She asks her other colleagues if they have observed the same behavior, and they indicate they have. The teacher contacts the parents and asks them, "I notice Kim has been sleeping in class. He sleeps each morning when he comes in. He sometimes wakes up during our second period, around 10 a.m., but he

does not participate in class activities. Sometimes when I ask him to participate, he raises his voice at me. I know this is not like Kim's typical behavior. Is there anything that you're aware of that might be causing this?" This way of phrasing it allows both teachers and family to problem solve, understanding the issue at hand rather than being blocked by one's own preconceptions from seeing the issue correctly.

The first step in being able to support your students is having an accurate understanding of their needs, their strengths, and their responses in the classroom, seeing behaviors accurately prior to drawing inferences. To understand each of these, without "interference" from one's own perceptions, expectations, or prior experience, teachers must state exactly what they see—no more, no less—and then identify potential reasons for the behavior only after they are sure that it has been accurately described.

What is a behavioral observation?

Behavioral observation may entail watching children at play in order to gain a sense of their motor skills, social skills, and response to unstructured or free time.

The term *behavioral observation* is one that is widely used in psychology and in assessment. Frequently, the term is used to denote a protocol for assessment based on behaviors that are recorded by an observer and later analyzed. In the literature, behavioral observation is often discussed as a component of psychiatric or educational evaluation and may focus on specific behaviors in order to evaluate (Nock & Kurtz, 2005). As we use the term, in relation to classroom teachers who observe students and describe student learning every day, we define it as follows: A behavioral observation is a record of what you see or hear, documented by describing (either verbally or in writing) exactly what it was that you saw or heard, in such as way that those who read or hear your observation will understand exactly what you saw or heard as though they had been there. In other words, there is *no indication of your interpretation* or perceptions. When recording factual statements, a behavioral observation uses quotation marks to record what was heard and avoids interpretive description or inference.

Consider the two examples in Figure 4.1.

Figure 4.1   Correctly and Incorrectly Phrased Behavioral Observations, Examples 1 and 2

Example 1: Correctly Phrased Behavioral Observation

The room was set up so that there were rows of six desks going horizontally across the room and eight desks going from the front of the room to the back, for a total of 48 desks in the classroom. Yolanda's desk is in the second row, third from the window. Juan, who Yolanda had introduced at the beginning of class as her "next door neighbor in the apartment building," sits at the table on Yolanda's left. Maria, a friend of Yolanda's since preschool, sits at the desk on her right. The blinds are pulled, covering the windows. When the teacher pulled the blinds at the start of class, she had indicated, "It will help you see the board better if the sun is not producing a glare." The teacher stood in front of the class. She had a picture of a sample drawing taped to the blackboard and she told the children to look at it as she explained the directions. The classroom bell was on the ceiling above Yolanda's desk. The physical education room was directly above Yolanda's classroom. As the teacher spoke, one could hear what the teacher said "sounded like balls bouncing and children running across the floor overhead." The teacher told the students that the heat was turned off so that they could keep their outside coats or sweaters on.

Example 2: Incorrectly Phrased Behavioral Observation

The room was set up in a traditional manner. There were many desks in the crowded room. *(Traditional for what culture? What grade? What school? For what activities? How many children and desks were there? What size was the room?)* Yolanda sat toward the middle of the room toward the front of the class. *(This isn't telling you exactly where she sat or her relationship to others around her.)* The room was dark. *(Tell why? What did you see? Were there no light bulbs? Was it late in the day? Was it a stormy, cloudy day?)* The teacher stood in the front of the room and gave directions. *(Verbally? With illustration, or did she demonstrate? Were they written?)* There seemed to be a lot of potential for noise as the gym was on the floor above the class and the classroom bell was on the ceiling. *(You can't observe potential for noise. If you mean to say that you actually heard noise, say so.)* Since it was cold, most of the children wore their coats or sweaters. *(How is "cold" measured? Does that mean there was snow in the room? That the window was open on a day when the temperature was 40 degrees? Does it mean that the windows were broken and snow was blowing into the classroom?)*

In Figure 4.1, Example 2 (Incorrectly Phrased Behavioral Observation), the observer has moved to making inferences, rather than providing facts or describing the student's behaviors. As you read through this example, take time to review the questions in parentheses at various points in the paragraph. These questions indicate areas where the observation should be—and is not—phrased behaviorally. They also make clear the impact of nonbehavioral statements: The reader is not able to draw conclusions but must rely on the observer's inferences and hope that they are indeed accurate! In this case, as you can see, the two observations have a very different tone and provide a different picture of Yolanda.

As you read through each hypothetical observation, you may notice obvious differences between the two written observations. An individual trying to craft an intervention to support Yolanda—or even trying to provide general suggestions and strategies to the classroom teacher—might have a far easier time working with the first set of statements in Example 1 (Correctly Phrased

Behavioral Observation), as the antecedent for Yolanda's behavior, and the components of her behavior, are clearly stated. This makes it easier to isolate the issues that might be causing Yolanda difficulty in order to address them. As Example 1 demonstrates, the ability to "see" accurately, and to report what one sees rather than one's interpretations or inferences, makes a difference in how the situation appears to others who may read or hear your account. By reporting events behaviorally, you make it possible for others to understand the full sequence and range of the student's behavior and, even more important, to identify appropriate interventions based on what actually occurs—not based on one's biases and preconceptions.

In the example that opened this chapter, Oliver, the student who was referred for special education services had already been labeled "resistant," and that label, we would argue, prevented his teachers from seeing his situation and his needs as clearly as they could have. Behavioral phrasing might have helped them state their concerns in a way that led them to consider the impact of outside factors (such as medication), rather than predetermining the cause of his issues to be his own "resistance" or "behavior problems."

What does a behavioral observation describe?

A behavioral observation can describe the setting, time frame, and environmental conditions as well as the behavior of the individual being observed. In Figure 4.2, the observer's statement of events in behavioral terms makes a significant difference in terms of allowing the reader to understand what occurred and what might help to address the causes. In particular, in the "incorrectly phrased" example (Example 4), the observer has moved to making inferences, rather than providing facts or describing the student's behaviors—with the result that a reader would have difficulty in accurately understanding exactly what occurred in the classroom. The paired observations in Figure 4.2 (which again follow the "correct-incorrect" format) focus again on Yolanda's classroom; they provide some further insight into the environmental conditions and other factors that may influence the teacher's instruction and the students' learning outcomes.

Figure 4.2 Correctly and Incorrectly Phrased Behavioral Observations, Examples 3 and 4

Example 3: Correctly Phrased Behavioral Observation

Yolanda sat in her chair, facing the teacher, who stood in the front of the room. As the teacher distributed the crayons, Yolanda put her head on the desk and shut her eyes. As the teacher approached Yolanda's desk, the teacher bent down, putting her head close to Yolanda's ear and (inaudibly to the observer) said something to Yolanda, whose eyes remained shut. Yolanda did not move but stated, in a voice that attracted the turning heads of the remaining 20 children in the room who stared at her as she screamed, "You can't make me color. I hate coloring. Besides, I am not good at staying in the lines!"

Example 4: Incorrectly Phrased Behavioral Observation

Yolanda was paying attention to the teacher until the teacher finished talking. *(What did you see that led you to this inference? How do you know she was paying attention?)* Then Yolanda got tired and put her head down. The teacher thought that Yolanda was withdrawing from the classroom activity. *(You can't tell what someone thought simply by looking at her. What did Yolanda do that was interpreted as "withdrawal"?)* Seeing Yolanda with her head down, the teacher got angry and walked towards Yolanda's desk. *(What did the teacher do that led you to infer that she was angry? State those actions, instead of your inference or interpretation of what you saw.)* Yolanda pretended to be asleep and not hear the teacher approaching. *(How do you know she really heard the teacher approaching? Can you see that? How do you know that she was pretending to be asleep? Perhaps she was tired or afraid of the teacher—each of those inferences might be equally plausible. Why focus on just one?)* Yolanda was furious and yelled at the top of her lungs causing the other children to turn in fear. *(How do you know Yolanda couldn't yell louder? How do you know the children in the class were scared? There are other reasons they could have looked.)* Yolanda told the teacher she wasn't going to do the coloring at all because she didn't do anything that she wasn't good at. *(What did Yolanda say that told you she thought she wasn't good at coloring? State it.)*

As one might notice, the two accounts—one correctly phrased and one incorrectly phrased—both provide a different view of the classroom environment, which can in turn influence teacher and student actions. Consider the differences between the two, and use the chart in Figure 4.3 to note at least five ways in which those differences might influence a teacher's perception of the situation and the students.

Why perform behavioral observations?

A behavioral observation can be performed for any one (or more) of several reasons:

- To document a student's academic or socioemotional growth over time
- To identify strengths and needs in order to facilitate further instruction
- To determine whether specific target behaviors are present or not (for example, observing to determine whether a student stays awake during class, or to determine whether a student is completing math problems on the level indicated by the county curriculum)
- To describe the frequency, intensity, and duration of students' behaviors (for example, to determine the frequency of self-stimulatory activities performed by a student with an autism spectrum disorder) in order to identify those that do not contribute to student's development and develop a plan to reduce them
- To facilitate increased social or academic development by identifying environmental factors that may be conducive or may not be conducive to development

Depending on the needs of the child, it is possible that one observation may serve more than one of the purposes listed. While this list represents some

Figure 4.3   Interventions Based on Observations

"Incorrect" Version Says	Interventions or Follow-Up That May Be Selected Based on Statements	"Correct" Version Says	Interventions or Follow-Up That May Be Selected Based on Statements
1.			
2.			
3.			
4.			
5.			

common reasons for conducting behavioral observation, it is not exhaustive. You may come across other reasons, equally valid, for engaging in behavioral observation.

In fact, it is our belief that behavioral observation is not a one-shot deal. Teachers should make a habit of looking at students behaviorally, of describing student outcomes in behavioral terms, and of "thinking" behaviorally—making inferences or judgments only after carefully examining the observed evidence. For that reason, we consider this chapter to be a guide to behavioral thinking as well as the procedure of behavioral observation. The skill of thinking behaviorally is, indeed, one that is developed over time and through reflective practice—with or without the use of any specific observation form.

What is an inference, and how is it different from an observation?

An inference is a judgment about what one observes. It is an attempt to interpret what one saw or heard so as to reach conclusions that will facilitate teaching. An observation is not an inference—observation must come before inference, and each observation can lead to multiple inferences.

Why is it important for teachers to differentiate inferences from observational data?

Teachers must be able to clearly identify the behavior demonstrated in their classrooms prior to drawing inferences for a number of reasons. These reasons are listed below:

It is essential to observe even while teaching. Identify your purpose in advance, and give yourself an opportunity to record your observations during breaks in the lesson.

- To provide specific observable and measurable information. This information can lead to several differing inferences. Jumping to inferences or conclusions (the why of the behavior) without further checking out your hypothesis (through further observations and assessment) may lead to the wrong conclusions and result in inappropriate instruction, selection of materials, grouping, and so on.
- To identify the antecedent to behaviors in order to discern what is occurring prior to the observed behavior, and thus increase the likelihood of change.

- To examine that behavior in light of culture; gender; expectations; background; and racial, linguistic, class, or ethnic diversity; and prior to drawing inferences.
- To examine the behavior in light of possible disability, developmental delay, or other physiological factors.

It is important to clearly state the observed behavior before going on to make inferences, as one fact or behavior can lead to multiple observations and also to multiple inferences. Each of these might, on its own merits, seem plausible; determining which one is the accurate one requires careful consideration of other factors (familial, social, environmental, physiological, cultural, linguistic, and academic, for example).

Each of the hypothetical reasons in Figure 4.4 might explain the behavior described at the beginning of the chart. As always, further observation is likely needed to determine which of the many choices might be most appropriate. In a classroom, it is not advisable to draw inferences based on a one-shot, brief observation. To be more accurate in drawing inferences, one should have observed the same person, in the same setting, over a period of time in order to identify whether or not the behavior is patterned, stable, and predictable—part of the individual's ongoing "typical" responses.

Having considered the distinction between observation and inference, the next step is to consider what follows inference. Once you have drawn an inference, and supported it with observational data, then you likely will want to consider what interventions might support the student's success, based on the

---

Figure 4.4 Multiple Inferences From One Observation

Observation: The girl did not look at the teacher as he introduced the topic of chemistry. Her eyes were cast down toward the floor.

Potential Inferences

1. The girl is not interested in the lesson.

2. The girl is hearing impaired and does not know the teacher was speaking.

3. The girl is from a culture that teaches that it is disrespectful to look directly into the eyes of an elder or an authority figure.

4. The girl is visually distracted, so she tends to compensate by focusing on auditory stimuli (listening without making eye contact).

5. The girl is not feeling well.

6. The girl has been emotionally traumatized by events she witnessed in her home country, in the process of journeying to the United States, or in her family or community since arrival, and she is not ready to focus on issues of academics.

7. The girl has a processing problem and does not make meaning out of what she hears.

8. The girl has never been in a school in this country or culture before and has not learned school expectations to demonstrate "listening."

9. The girl doesn't speak or understand English.

inference you made. For example, imagine that you see a student putting his head down in class. After investigating the student's home life further, you draw the inference that the student is tired from staying up with his baby brother all night while his parent was working a late shift at the local factory. In considering appropriate interventions, you would likely speak to the counselor about connecting the student's family with resources and support, provide the student opportunities to review schoolwork that he missed while sleeping, and work with the student to ensure his homework was completed (perhaps during lunch or after school, so that he did not have to worry about it when going home for the evening to what amounted to another full-time, child-care job).

When considering the degree of intervention needed in response to a given behavior, consider the impact of the behavior. Is the behavior getting in the way of learning? A student may be sitting with one leg tucked under during a silent reading session. Some teachers we know would consider this a violation of classroom rules that require students to sit with both feet on the floor or to turn their body straight ahead in the chair. While not the most "orthopedically correct" option, this posture is not disrupting the student or peers. In fact, it may very well help the student to concentrate. Therefore, we would not recommend addressing the student's posture with behavioral or instructional interventions (unless, of course, the student has a health issue, communicated by family members or school health staff, which makes it undesirable to sit in that fashion).

NEW STEPS TO TAKE—TOMORROW

1. Accurately "see" your students.

The ability to phrase an observation behaviorally is a skill that is gained with practice. Plan to spend some time in the next few days engaging in careful observation of your classroom, and ideally of one or two particular students, in order to record your observations using behavioral phrasing.

Consider the behaviors, activities, and learning outcomes of those students in response to their environment, demands placed upon them, interpersonal skills and dynamics within the classroom, social and emotional challenges, and prior knowledge. You may wish to take the classroom observation guide (see Figure 4.5) with you to observe your students in a setting where you are not typically with them (so that you can focus on observation rather than on your instructional duties): the playground, the gym, or the art classroom. Record your observations on this template, and fill in your inferences and conclusions only after carefully considering the context and impact of the behaviors you observe.

How to Use This Information

The information recorded in Figure 4.5 is helpful in two ways. First, it can serve as a guide to let you know how your behavioral-observation skills are developed (or where you might want to invest more time in practicing behavioral statements). Consider sharing your observation with colleagues and asking them to provide feedback on your work. Explain to them that your

Figure 4.5 Classroom-Observation Guide

Behavioral-Observation Guide

Class:

Student:

Date:

Location:

From: To:

Observations (These may include elements relating to instruction.)

- What do you see and hear in the classroom?
- What does the student say? What do others say to the student?
- What is the physical environment of the classroom like?

Impact of Behaviors Observed (Stated Behaviorally)

- Impact on school routine
- Impact on student's academic success
- Impact on social and emotional well-being
- Impact on interpersonal relationships

Inferences Regarding Behaviors and Potential Interventions

goal is to create a behavioral observation, stating what is seen rather than judging or assigning any kind of value or blame to the actions observed. Sometimes a second reader can point out any areas where your statements could be clarified or made more objective.

Second, this information can also help you to identify behaviors that you would like to target in one or more of your students. You may consider targeting either positive behaviors—which you would reinforce with positive feedback—or negative behaviors—which you would address through a variety of interventions. Review your notes; then, consider which behaviors seem to be having an impact on students' learning, engagement, socioemotional well-being, or safety. If you have not done so yet, note these behaviors in the second area of the chart, under your observations.

Finally, consider the context of the behaviors in order to make appropriate and supported inferences regarding what you have seen. Can you identify a catalyst or cause for the behavior? Does it seem to recur at any point? You will note these ideas in the third area of the chart—but keep reading, first, in order to explore the concept of "context" in more depth.

2. Place your observations in context in order to interpret them.

When interpreting a child's behavior, consider the context in which the behavior occurs.

There is a myriad of factors that must be considered when one is trying to interpret observed behaviors. See Figure 4.6.

How to Use This Information

None of these concepts can be taken in isolation; while we (and others in the field) have created different categories of questions to facilitate analysis of the behavior, keep in mind that each of these categories has the potential to impact the others. Therefore, they must be examined holistically (rather than with respect to just one category). For example, the degree or intensity of a behavior may be a function of the setting the child is in. When might you see this in your classroom? Suppose one of your students has not formed strong social relationships with her peers. On a typical day, the student might spend much of her time sitting alone, in the back of the room, drawing and talking to herself rather than to peers. Suppose that in PE class, the class is asked to select one partner in order to complete a soccer drill. You

Observation has to occur within the context of one's knowledge of development and within a contextual frame of reference.

might conceivably see this student's behaviors change due to the stress of identifying and selecting a peer with whom she feels comfortable working. If the student were to look at the instructor and say, "No, I won't. You can't

Figure 4.6 Context: Identify Factors That May Influence Behavior

Contextual Factor	Questions to Ask	Your Notes
Setting	Where does the behavior occur? Are there specific times of day or places associated with the behavior?	
Degree	What is the intensity of the behavior? How does the degree of this behavior correspond to the degree of the student's typical behavior? Where does this behavior fall along the range of typical responses for a student of this particular age, skill level, and so on?	
Frequency	How often does a behavior occur? Is it repeated or a one-shot deal? Does it occur more or less frequently in response to specific settings?	
Relationships	With what person or groups of people does the behavior occur? Or is the behavior unrelated to the dynamics of relationships? What reactions do others have to the behavior? How does the behavior impact relationships with others?	
Antecedent	Is the behavior a response to a particular event, situation, person, place, or thing?	

make me pick a partner!" her response would certainly be considered to be atypical for the circumstances. However, when considered in light of the child's social and emotional needs and state, the behavior might appear less atypical or more predictable. The escalation in *degree* (from quietly sitting and ignoring the class, to actively defying the instructor) can be seen as being (at least in part) a function of the change in setting and interpersonal relationship demands that the student encountered.

You may find, as you continue to consider the concept, that you can identify examples that are even more pertinent to your individual students and to your specific classroom. As you continue to consider your observations and your students' behaviors, keep the context in mind—an accurate view of context is necessary to ensure your inferences are well-grounded and supported by fact.

Once you have identified potential factors related to the behavior, the final step involves targeting specific behaviors, as appropriate, through interventions.

A Word About Interventions

Intervention has become a sort of buzzword in recent years, particularly with the development of approaches such as RTI (response to intervention), which seek to implement targeted interventions based on an evaluation of the child's needs and to track data to determine the efficacy of the intervention. We applaud the development and adoption of such approaches. We also believe that interventions must be targeted and appropriate to each student's needs, based upon a thorough, behavioral assessment that takes related factors and context into account. More and more frequently, schools may adopt a specific intervention (such as a selected phonics program), which is provided to any and all students who exhibit a given difficulty. Such approaches may not help students and are not likely to be as effective as those in which interventions are tailored to each particular student based on a careful analysis of the individual's needs.

Observation can entail ongoing documentation of behavior to identify patterns in students' social, emotional, and academic responses.

3. Select and Implement Appropriate Interventions

What is an intervention?

An intervention is an action that you, as the teacher, perform in response to the observed behavior and the inference you decided was most likely to be accurate.

For instance, let's return to the example given earlier in the chapter, in Figure 4.4, of the girl who was not making eye contact with her teacher. If you concluded the girl was not looking at the teacher because she was not interested in the material, one possible intervention might be to teach the subject matter by tying it to a particular interest of hers. If the girl liked candy, one such way would be to demonstrate what happens to chocolate and sugar when they are heated or cooled to different states. Another way to procure her investment might be to have her work with a small group of friends to identify substances used in their daily lives that are presented or used as a solid, liquid, or gas.

If, on the other hand, the girl's failure to make eye contact were due to cultural reasons, then the interventions used would be very different. First, one would have to decide whether the goal of requiring the student to make eye contact was appropriate for the student at that stage in her development, acculturation, and educational career. There are certainly arguments for helping students to adjust to the expectations of American culture (so that eventually students learn to feel more comfortable making eye contact, as that is often an expectation in the American school and work environments). However, there are also powerful arguments for doing so gradually, once the child has had an opportunity to fully acculturate and to feel comfortable adopting elements of American culture. This may or may not be appropriate in the student's high school science class, depending on the student's relationship with the teacher, number of months or years in the country, and relationships with others in the school. It may be that a trusted teacher, counselor, ESOL (English for speakers of other languages) teacher, or other school personnel with a strong personal relationship to the student is the best individual to present information about American norms related to school culture.

As indicated in the sidebar (A Word About Interventions on p. 61), the concept of interventions is not a new one. However, our concern with interventions here involves two important concepts.

First, one size does not fit all when it comes to interventions. For example, the same phonemic awareness program is not likely to be an appropriate intervention for every third grader (or ninth grader!) who exhibits reading difficulties.

Second, each intervention must be tailored to the student's age, cultural and linguistic background, level of socioeconomic development, current skills, and cognitive and academic development. An elaboration on the theme of "one size fits all," this principle is further illustrated with the intervention guide in Figure 4.8.

Selecting Appropriate Interventions: The Questions

When you set out to perform a behavioral observation, the questions in Figure 4.7 are among those you may want to address. We have grouped these in areas that pertain to what might commonly be seen in the classroom. The

Figure 4.7 Factors to Consider While Performing a Behavioral Observation

Area of Instruction	Key Questions	Your Notes
Classroom environment	What was the physical layout of the room? What was the grouping of desks? Where did the student sit? Did the student sit near others who appeared to be friendly toward him or her? Was the classroom warm or cold? What kind of background noise, if any, was present? How close together were the desks or tables?	
Context for learning	What was the objective for the day? How did the teacher connect this objective to prior learning or prior knowledge? Did the teacher preassess for background knowledge before beginning instruction? If so, how did the student perform on the preassessment? How did the teacher respond to the results of the preassessment? Was the student ready for the lesson to begin, with materials and supplies available if they were needed? Did the teacher give directions as to what materials were needed?	
Classroom management	Did it appear that routines and procedures were in place? Did it appear that students were aware of routines, procedures, and consequences? Were class expectations posted in a visible location in the classroom? Did the student comply with all routines and expectations, some, or none? How did the teacher respond to students who did not comply? Did other students comply with all rules, some, or none?	
Teacher questioning and interaction	What questions or prompts did the teacher use to elicit student responses? Did the teacher "shelter" content or questions at all by using simplified vocabulary, or explaining vocabulary, if needed? How did the teacher respond to students' answers (both correct and incorrect)? What types of questioning strategies did the teacher use? Did teacher-student interaction occur within the context of whole-class instruction, small-group instruction, independent work, or all three? Did the teacher take steps to ensure all students understood directions before beginning an activity? If so, how? Did the teacher check for understanding?	
Student responses	How did students respond to prompts, activities, and teacher questions? Did the student respond in a manner similar to classmates, or in a different manner? Did the student complete all activities? Did the student follow directions? If not, did the student indicate a reason ("I don't understand," for example)?	
Assessment	What was the summative assessment for the lesson? Was it aligned to the objective? Did the teacher formatively assess student progress throughout the lesson to ensure students would be able to complete the summative assessment? How did the student perform on the summative assessment? On the formative assessment? Did the individual indicate understanding throughout the lesson by responding to teacher questions, completing activities, or asking questions?	

questions may help to guide your thinking, not only as you observe, but also as you review your observation data in order to select appropriate interventions.

How to Use This Information

Once you complete an observation and begin to draw conclusions or inferences, your next step will be to identify interventions that you believe best meet your student or students' needs. Selecting the intervention, of course, is only the beginning; you will also continue to assess its effectiveness as you implement it. It is likely that your school or district has a process in place for implementing and monitoring interventions as part of a tiered intervention program or RTI process. If not, or if you are implementing interventions informally in your own classroom before referring a student for team-based support, you may want to review the following steps to be sure that your process incorporates some necessary elements: selection, implementation, review and progress monitoring (reviewing your data to see whether the student appears to be making progress), and evaluation of the intervention.

The process of selecting an appropriate intervention requires consistent implementation and review to ensure that the intervention is actually impacting the needs that have been identified. The list in Figure 4.8 provides the steps involved in selecting and implementing interventions based on behavioral observations.

Figure 4.8 The Process of Selecting Appropriate Interventions

1. Behavioral observation

2. Identification of student's needs

3. Brainstorming or survey of available resources to identify appropriate intervention

4. Selection of appropriate intervention

5. Implementation and data collection

6. Monitoring of student's progress (reviewing collected data on a regular basis to determine whether student is moving toward goals)

7. Analysis of effectiveness (should include cross-checking against needs that were originally identified through observation and/or other needs assessments)

How to Use This Information

The process of selecting and appropriately implementing interventions can be carried out in the classroom by a single teacher. However, it is far more often carried out in collaboration with others. You may wish to begin by checking this list (see Figure 4.8) against the process that is currently in place (either in your school or in your own classroom) and discussing any variances with the colleagues with whom you work most closely. Consider using Figure 4.9 as you observe your students and decide what will work best for them. You may find this sample chart useful to use in jotting your notes.

Figure 4.9 Recording and Reflecting on Observations and Goals

Student Name:	Grade Level:
Information	**My Ideas**
Student's identified needs	
Interventions appropriate for needs	
Effectiveness of interventions as implemented (based on data collected over time)	
"Match" or "mismatch" between results and needs originally identified	
Results of follow-up behavioral observation to determine needs have been met	
Follow-up ideas	

The chart (see Figure 4.9) is not meant to replace your school's formal processes for recording data during the progress monitoring phase of the intervention. Rather, it should serve as a vehicle for you to record your own observations regarding the "fitness" or "match" of the intervention to the needs that you originally identified through behavioral observation. You may choose to share your notes with others—or to keep them as private jottings to help you sort out your own "take" on the intervention process. Either way, the key point is that the interventions must match the needs that you originally identified through behavioral observation. Later, in Chapter 9, we will discuss more fully the process of collaborating to implement interventions for student success, building on the information provided here.

SUMMARY

The process of behavioral observation is central to identifying appropriate interventions, with full awareness of the cultural, linguistic, etiological, social, and emotional needs of the child and the way in which those may impact performance in the classroom. Behavioral observation is the first step in a process that involves making appropriate inferences about students' needs, based on observed data, and culminates in the selection of interventions that are appropriate to the needs observed. Further behavioral observation should be a key part of the evaluation process in order to determine whether interventions are working or not. Information gained from observations may be shared with your colleagues, as interventions often are implemented within a collaborative framework.

EXTENSION AND COLLABORATION

1. Consider sharing this information: Ask a colleague, first, to review behavioral-observation procedures with you and, second, to conduct a behavioral observation within your classroom. Offer to do the same in your colleague's classroom as well, and then share your observations.

2. Once you feel comfortable with the concept of behavioral observation (and perhaps you already do), offer to share one or two suggestions at a team meeting or a meeting of the school's prereferral committee. You may even decide to volunteer to serve on the committee.

3. The role of cultural and linguistic variables is particularly important when observing CLD (culturally and linguistically diverse) students and crafting appropriate interventions. Select one of your current students and identify one or two areas where the student's culture or language may have had an impact on some of the observed classroom behaviors— either behaviors that support learning or behaviors that hinder learning. Share your observations with one or two colleagues who teach the same student.

NEXT STEPS

As you consider how to use behavioral observation as a tool in your classroom, it is likely that you will find yourself giving increased attention to the full spectrum of students' needs—including social, emotional, and mental wellness issues. Chapter 5 addresses some of these issues at length, providing an overview of mental wellness and its importance in the classroom and school settings. As you read, consider the ways in which that information about mental wellness can influence the inferences that are drawn in the classroom by teachers conducting behavioral observations.

COMMUNITY CONNECTIONS

1. One benefit of behavioral observation is that it allows us to look beyond biases or preconceptions to identify areas of success or strength in students who may not have previously met with school success. Identify one such student in your class. Observe the student, and note at least one behavior that is beneficial to the student or the class. Write the student's parents a note (or make a phone call) to praise the student. (If the student is an English language learner, you may consider asking your school system's Language Line or translation service to help you with conveying the information.)

2. Think about the needs that you identified in your students. Identify one such need, and research community organizations that exist to meet that need. Ask the organization to provide you literature or information that you can share at your next staff meeting. For example, for students with behavioral or emotional disabilities, your local hospital or mental health center may be able to provide specific strategies for working with adolescents. If students' socioeconomic needs make it difficult for them to access the curriculum in the same manner other students do, your local social services agency, or a private relief agency, may be able to provide information on connecting families with needed resources.

USEFUL WEBSITES

- State and District Websites on RTI and Progress Monitoring. In Chapter 9, we recommend several websites on RTI and collaboration. However, as you work on refining your own observation skills in order to identify appropriate interventions for your students, we recommend taking some time to acquaint yourself with the resources that are already in place for your district or state. Most states, and many districts, are at least beginning the process of building frameworks for tiered interventions. As part of this process, many have developed (or are developing) guides for observation, intervention, and data collection. We encourage you to make some time to explore and access those resources. You might begin by speaking to your school's special education personnel or administrators, as they might be able to point you to some useful sites and suggest some local resources that would be helpful.

5 Mental Wellness and Students' Resiliency

Making School an Emotionally Safe Place

L uis is a ninth grader who was born and raised in the United States. His parents immigrated to the United States before he was born. Halfway through the school year, Luis's teachers began to notice that his attitude and behaviors in the classroom were changing. Luis has become hostile and verbally aggressive toward his peers and his teachers and often walks in several minutes late to class without an excuse or apology. When working in groups with his peers, he frequently starts and engages in conflicts with them and, at times, even refuses to work in groups with students who have previously appeared to be his friends. Luis has also been observed sitting alone during lunch time and alone in the halls between classes, isolated from his group of friends. When speaking to the school counselor, one of Luis's friends indicated that Luis's father, who had been an unauthorized resident in the United States ever since his visa expired twelve years previously, was recently detained in an immigration detention center and is currently awaiting a deportation hearing.

THE ISSUES

- Definitions of *mental wellness* and its impact on school success
- Staff awareness of students' personal circumstances
- Impact on school success of stress, trauma, family situation, students' experiences, and acculturation
- Student resiliency and strategies to foster it
- Issues impacting students' availability to discuss personal emotional, social, or familial challenges that they may be facing
- Effective supports for students who are at risk for mental wellness difficulties

QUESTIONS TO CONSIDER

1. What issues might be impacting Luis's success in school?

2. Luis has chosen to confide in his counselor. What are the school's and district's legal mandates and policies for the manner in which sensitive information is (or is not) shared with other school personnel or reported?

3. What supports might the school provide for Luis and his family?

4. How can his teachers provide support to Luis and communicate that they are available, acknowledge the reality of his life, and therefore "free him up" to learn?

GETTING THE ANSWERS

School professionals, as well as those within the general health community, have long recognized the need for mental health awareness and support (U.S. Department of Health and Human Services [USDHHS], 1999; National Association of School Psychologists, 2009). The U.S. Surgeon General, in 1999, defined *mental health* as "a state of successful performance of mental function, resulting in productive activities, fulfilling relationships with other people, and the ability to change and cope with adversity" (USDHHS, 1999, p. vii).

This definition, like all definitions, is culturally bound and, in practice, its interpretation is culturally mediated (Vygotsky, 1978). As discussed in Chapter 4, accurate observations (rather than inferences) are crucial to understanding what "successful performance" in any area constitutes. This is particularly the case when attempting to measure categories such as "mental function," "productivity," or "fulfilling relationships." What defines productivity? Who decides if a relationship is fulfilling? In coping with adversity, what cultural framework and values are used to guide decisions and to determine the best method of handling adverse events?

It is important, first of all, for school and mental health professionals to be aware of this cultural context as they consider the presence (or absence) of mental health in their students. Not every culture sees mental wellness in the same way, nor does every culture take a similar view of the role mental wellness may play in educational well-being and success. Mental health and wellness issues are often considered to exist most frequently within a medical-clinical model, where the focus is on the diagnosis and treatment of specific conditions. However, mental wellness, as defined by the U.S. Department of Health and Human Services (1999), incorporates a broader view of an individual's needs and functioning, as well as the factors that may influence them. In school settings, this involves looking at students' family lives, prior experiences, cultural and linguistic background, and other factors, as well as their experiences within school. Students, particularly those who are culturally and linguistically diverse (CLD), must negotiate their past experiences, face uncertainty about the present and future, and still function appropriately within the daily demands of the school setting. This is a challenging task for anyone—but for students whose prior experiences or current situations involve exceptional stressors, such as recent trauma, prior school challenges, family separation, socioeconomic stress, and the like, it requires a tremendous amount of energy and resiliency. Students struggle to resolve the immediate and long-term impact of challenging personal and family circumstances—they may not be able to appreciate their teachers' exhortations that doing homework tonight will allow them to get a diploma, go on to college, receive a lucrative job offer, and so on. Students may, understandably, be much more focused on survival—their own or family members'—and students may, also, be struggling with the impact of adjustment to a new land and culture. Some teachers of our acquaintance, in fact, speak of the cultural "custody battles" experienced by students, a phrase that accurately captures the stress and pressure that may face students who are navigating between a prior or native culture and the new culture of U.S. society and the American educational system.

The Surgeon General's report continues: "Mental health [wellness] is indispensable to personal well-being, family and interpersonal relationships, and contribution to community or society . . . . Mental health is the springboard of thinking and communication skills, learning, emotional growth, resilience, and self-esteem" (USD-HHS, 1999, p. ix). Again, this definition both clarifies the importance of mental health and wellness and, also, points out a number of categories where perceptions of mental health can be very much determined by one's cultural frame of reference, socioeconomic state, prior experiences, or other factors. When perceiving the success of "family and interpersonal relationships" (or attempting to infer the way in which a student's mental wellness has impacted such relationships), one's own beliefs and attitudes have the potential to color the inferences or the conclusions that are drawn. The same potential for misinterpretation exists when analyzing other variables, including learning, emotional growth, self-esteem, and the like. First and foremost, it is useful to remember that mental health and wellness must be interpreted within the context of each student's family situation, needs, strengths, and experiences.

A framework for addressing mental wellness involves considering students' overall self-concept, including elements such as ability to engage in play, social and emotional context, and availability to learn.

Second, issues such as mental health and wellness can, when misinterpreted, frequently feed into a "deficit" model focused on the needs and challenges facing CLD students. It is true that CLD students, for reasons associated with familial, linguistic, and acculturation variables, may be at risk for particular challenges both within the school setting and outside it. These challenges are not limited to the CLD population, but may occur in greater frequency insofar as they are linked to, for example, second-language acquisition, acculturation, trauma, family separation, and socioeconomic challenge (Mazur & Givens, 2004). However, we believe it is important to focus not on the potential negatives but on the resiliency and strength that enable students faced with these challenges to persevere and succeed in school. For that reason, we believe it is as important to focus on mental and emotional strength and wellness as it is to focus on the potential challenges that exist to mental wellness. Because the term *mental health* is frequently used in conjunction with discussion of specific challenges and difficulties, we prefer to use the term *mental wellness* as we believe it conveys a focus on the positive aspects of mental functioning that make it possible for all students to succeed despite whatever challenging circumstances may present themselves.

Nevertheless, school success is impacted by external variables, particularly language learning; acculturation; and adjustment to a new country, culture, school, family separation, and trauma (Mazur & Givens, 2004). For CLD students—many of whom are new to the United States and are learning a second language and navigating a new culture, or are coping with family separation and the absence of parents and siblings—this may be the case. Each of these variables can produce stress, which serves to increase the strain that may already be in place due to trauma, adjustment, or acculturation issues. In addition, each of these factors can combine with stress to create or intensify the effects of conditions such as depression or anxiety (American Psychological Association, 2003). It is also possible that students from diverse backgrounds—as well as many of those native to the United States—may have been raised in situations where the cultural context does not incorporate the American medical-clinical approach to diagnosing and treating mental health issues—or where the socioeconomic status of the family does not provide students with readily available access to mental wellness care. This can lead to situations where students and family members may not be aware of underlying mental health issues or may have strong feelings about proposed treatment methods. Here, too, cultural sensitivity is called for. It is problematic, from the perspective of cultural responsiveness and diversity awareness, for school personnel to force diagnosis and treatment on students and families who do not see those as appropriate steps. At the same time, it is important for school personnel to be aware of the signs of mental wellness challenges, so they can collaborate to offer appropriate in-school support and to refer families to out-of-school support services where appropriate.

Given the complexity of the issues surrounding mental wellness, school personnel must have a variety of skill sets related to the issue. For example, school staff must be able to

- Identify the factors that can contribute to mental wellness challenges for students

- Recognize potential signs indicating that students may need mental wellness support
- Collaborate with colleagues to provide appropriate support for students experiencing mental wellness challenges

Finally, school staff must be mindful of the legal and ethical context in which they operate. Mental wellness issues often fall under the purview of confidentiality regulations, as students may be sharing information that is sensitive and that needs to be treated in a confidential manner. Policies for staff may vary from district to district and even from state to state. We recommend that you speak with your guidance staff, and administrators, to determine the following:

- What type of information about my students should I share, or not share, with other teachers? What is the process for determining who "needs to know" a sensitive fact regarding a student (for example, a mental health issue or a recent change in family status)?
- What type of information can I expect a guidance counselor to share with me, if the counselor learns something about one of my students?
- In what situations should I refer a student to a counselor? What resources will be made available through the counselor?

NEW STEPS TO TAKE—TOMORROW

1. Recognize the factors that may impact your students' mental wellness, particularly for diverse learners.

The list in Figure 5.1 presents some of the issues that may impact mental wellness for diverse learners. This list places particular emphasis on challenges that may impact ELLs, as these may be the challenges least familiar to classroom teachers who have not had experience with many ELL students—and yet these may also be some of the most important issues to recognize in dealing with your ELL students. The research is clear that a child's mental wellness has much to do with school success, making this a crucial topic for teachers (Mazur & Givens, 2004). This list is subdivided into categories so that similar issues are grouped together. Based on the needs of your students, and their specific backgrounds, you may find specific sections of this list to be more or less relevant to the needs of your population.

How to Use This Information

This list (Figure 5.1) is meant to serve as a guide to help you identify specific issues that may relate to your students. Over time, research has demonstrated that students who face these issues may be at increased risk for mental wellness challenges, depending on the degree (severity) and frequency of occurrence and duration of the issues, as well as the support system available to help students cope. The emotional and psychological impact of any one of these factors

Figure 5.1	Acculturation and Adjustment Issues Facing Diverse Learners That May Impact Mental Wellness

- *Second-Language Acquisition.* The process of acquiring a second (or third, or fourth) language is itself stressful, cognitively and emotionally (Buttaro, 2002).
- *Literacy Demands.* As students move through various grade levels, the academic demands of school (and the demands of adapting to changing literacy demands of the school environment) become more rigorous—and potentially more stressful. This is particularly true for students who are still working to acquire reading proficiency on a level with their peers. In addition, literacy demands, like many elements of our educational system, are related to specific social and cultural beliefs and actions and are, also, deeply linked to questions of power, hierarchy, and values (cultural, familial, and individual) (Gee, 2000).
- *Variances in Norms for Interpersonal Communication.* These communication norms (particularly with authority figures) also may be culturally bound (Taylor, 1990).
- *School Routines and the Educational System Itself.* School and the school system may be structured differently, causing a challenge for students in the process of adjusting to the differences (Mazur & Givens, 2004).
- *Language Differences.* The transition to a new language, both social language and academic language, can be challenging and can make it difficult for students to access curriculum and feel that they "fit in" to their new school (Cummins, 1981).
- *Family Relationships and Availability.* Changes in family constellation can result from any number of factors, including deportation of relatives, family separation, and early emancipation due to absent parents. These changes can also present a challenge for ELLs who are navigating the adult world while also trying to still fulfill school responsibilities (Mazur & Givens, 2004).
- *Family Background and Educational Experience.* Educational backgrounds of family members may be different from those that are "typical" in a given community or school, leading to assumptions about common understandings that may not be accurate (Baca & de Valenzuela, 2004).
- *Socioeconomic Stress.* Family members may lack secure employment or affordable housing, causing socioeconomic strain (National Center for Children in Poverty, 2003).
- *Increased Mobility.* Mobility rates for CLD students tend to be higher than for non-CLD students, for reasons linked to availability of employment and, sometimes, local political movements against immigrants (Mazur & Givens, 2004).
- *Access to Health and Wellness Care and Information.* CLD students may have limited access to health care and to information about physical and mental wellness (Adkins, Sample, & Birman, 1999; Isserlis, 2000). Health issues can impact performance in school and can also impact the availability of family members to provide support to students.
- *Trauma.* CLD students may be recovering from traumatic events that occurred prior to immigration, such as oppression, separation from family members, violence, war, torture, or political upheaval. Even after the fact, such issues can have an impact on a student's mental and emotional well-being and can place students at increased risk for post-traumatic stress disorder (PTSD) (Adkins, Sample, & Birman, 1999; Isserlis, 2000).

can cause mental health challenges to students already navigating a complex new reality in school. In addition, these factors rarely occur in isolation; typically, one can cause other factors to occur or intensify. For example, family separation may cause socioeconomic strain, which may cause difficulties in nutrition and physical well-being. Or prior exposure to traumatic events in a student's home country may impact both second-language acquisition and the student's ability to develop peer relationships in the new setting. For this reason, teachers need to be particularly careful to maintain the "whole child" approach discussed in Chapter 1 (Baca & de Valenzuela, 2004), remaining open to the possibility of multiple issues having an impact on a single child.

That being said, you might consider reviewing this list (see Figure 5.1) while keeping a particular student in mind, so you can identify which specific issues apply. You might also review it with respect to an entire class, thinking about how different issues may manifest themselves and how the support you offer, and the way in which you offer it, may differ from student to student. Consider reviewing this list with colleagues, asking them to share impressions about a particular student and then cross-checking their response with your own.

Finally, consider the background of the students and the community in which your school is located. You may find that a large group of students share similar backgrounds. For example, your community may house an unusually large number of refugee families—or perhaps, a factory in your town has recently closed, leaving a significant number of parents and family members unemployed. Being aware of the factors that can cause mental wellness challenges is an important step in recognizing potential signs of student difficulties.

2. Know the potential indicators that a student may need additional mental wellness support.

In addition to thinking about the factors that can cause mental wellness challenges, it is important for teachers to also be aware of the potential signs that a student may be experiencing increased difficulties connected to mental wellness.

Use this list (see Figure 5.2) as a guide to help you recognize the indicators that your students may be under stress, may need additional support, or may need specialized services. However, none of these signs can be interpreted within a vacuum—nor is it appropriate for teachers or school staff (except those who are psychologists or counselors) to try to affix a medical or clinical label to behavior, as they are not licensed to do so. (We believe strongly that teachers are not mental health practitioners, nor are they expected to function in that capacity.) In fact, issues of mental wellness are often erroneously "diagnosed" as being related to etiological or psychological conditions, where the issues in play may instead be any combination of factors (see Figure 5.2). Following the list, a short scenario is provided to facilitate discussion of appropriate ways to broach a concern with parents or other family members (see Case Study).

Again, depending on the degree and frequency of the issues present and the ramifications for the student, the school, and the family, mental wellness support may or may not be needed in addition to academic, social, behavioral, physiological and health-related, and other supports. This list (Figure 5.2) is not meant to be a diagnostic checklist; rather, it is a summary of factors that, taken together with the holistic picture of a student's well-being, may indicate a need for additional support in one or more areas. Mental wellness is one of those (many) areas worth considering; we tend to overlook those potential issues in favor of ones that may seem more immediately relevant to a school's frame of reference (academic success, for example, or identification for a learning disability).

Figure 5.2 Potential Indicators of a Student's Need for Mental Wellness Support

- Sudden change in academic performance
- Stress reactions exhibited in response to a student's process of adjusting to a new culture, country, or school (which may present as apparent fear, unease, or anger)
- Sudden change in behavior, interest, peer group, or academic performance
- Changes in attendance and lateness (particularly negative trends)
- Difficulty maintaining attention
- Difficulty interacting appropriately with others, particularly if dramatic negative trends in social interactions are present
- Changes in student's typical behavior with respect to class participation, engagement in activities, or completion of work
- Outward signs or expressions of physical pain, discomfort, abuse, or neglect
- Change in sleeping habits, either outside school (self-reported or reported by family members) or during school

Source: Mazur and Givens (2004).

How to Use This Information

These indicators (see Figure 5.2) must be considered within the cultural context and background of the student and family, as each of them has the potential to be misinterpreted based on cultural variance, linguistic difference, and similar factors. You may wish to review the information on behavioral observation and supporting inferences (provided in Chapter 4) as you consider this list.

Decreased levels of participation in class could indeed be an indicator of mental wellness concerns. They could also be an indicator that a student is struggling with content or has a medical—not a psychological—health concern that limits participation, or a nutritional issue that has the same effect. One teacher of our acquaintance, who taught third grade, identified a student for academic and psychological intervention based on a consistent pattern of behavioral outbursts and off-task behavior. It was only after writing the intervention plan that the teacher and her colleagues learned the student had an abscessed tooth that had gone untreated for the past three months. Once the child's parent was referred to a low-cost health clinic for evaluation and treatment, the behavioral issues disappeared almost immediately.

With that in mind, we provide a mini-case study. We suggest you use this scenario in conjunction with the list in Figure 5.2, so you can first identify potential concerns based on the behavior described, and then work with one or more colleagues to describe supports (within the school and within the community) that could help family members address the concerns listed. Keep in mind, again, that there is a difference between identifying areas of concern and making a diagnosis that you may not be qualified to make. Consider the most appropriate way to present your concerns to Miya's parents in the scenario that follows.

Case Study

Miya is a third-grade student whose parents are natives of Japan. While her parents are both employed and have been in the United States for over six years, Miya has recently exhibited a change in behavior in school. Her teachers are wondering what might be responsible for her changed behavior. They ask Miya's parents to attend a meeting and broach the topic after some initial introductions. Miya's third-grade teacher begins the conversation. Consider the two potential openers in Figure 5.3 that he might use, and analyze each with respect to behavioral phrasing.

As you may notice in Figure 5.3, the second response, while well-intentioned, is problematic in two respects. First, it does not solicit what might be valuable information from family members, who could provide clues as to reasons underlying the change in Miya's behavior. Second, it makes a diagnosis, and produces a label, which a teacher—or any school staff unlicensed in psychology or mental health services—is not qualified to make. The first response, in contrast, seeks to describe the problem, solicit input from family members, and move toward a solution where both teacher and family can share information in hopes of understanding the best way to provide Miya with the support she may need. The first response, also, does not pigeonhole Miya as a student with a mental wellness issue, thereby providing space for her parents to share information about other factors (physical, nutritional, familial, emotional, or social) that may be impacting her behavior.

3. Provide support to create an emotionally safe environment and foster development of students' resiliency.

Maslow's (1943) hierarchy places basic physical needs in a most important position, stating that physiological needs such as food and shelter take priority over all others. Once those needs are satisfied, needs such as safety and security can be met. Only when each of these needs has been met is an individual free to focus on emotional and psychological needs: love, esteem, and acceptance. It is when all of these needs are met that the individual is finally able to achieve "self-actualization" (Mazur & Givens, 2004).

Figure 5.3	Phrasing Concerns About Students' Mental Wellness

Behavioral Phrasing Identifying Area of Concern. "Since she returned from the holiday break, Miya's behavior is different. She does not play with peers during recess, and she no longer sits with her friends at lunch. During silent reading time, she often puts her head down and cries to herself. I am wondering if you have any ideas about what might have caused this change."

Inappropriate Attempt to Diagnose. "Since she returned from holiday break, Miya's behavior has changed significantly. She withdraws from her friends and cries often. She displays all of the symptoms of depression. Have you had her evaluated by a psychologist or counselor? I can refer you to someone if it would help."

Again, in reviewing this information, it is helpful to keep in mind the distinction between clinical psychological issues and the need for practices that foster mental wellness. While classroom teachers are limited in their ability to diagnose and treat specific psychological conditions, they are not limited in the ability to create a welcoming and emotionally safe classroom. Make sure your classroom is one in which students' diverse experiences are respected, divergent perspectives are valued, and assumptions about backgrounds are not made haphazardly.

Family context and the availability of schools and teachers for family contact can be crucial elements in students' academic success and mental wellness.

What exactly do we mean by "assumptions about backgrounds"? Consider the following example: One school of our acquaintance held a celebration some years ago for parents. The students made cards, special crafts, and decorations for a lunch with their mother or father. One student, who had no living parents, approached her teacher and whispered in her ear, "Can I bring my older sister instead?" At that time, the school's policy, unfortunately, restricted the event to biological or adoptive parents only. The student was told that her sister could not attend and that she would need to find a friend who had two parents present and would be willing to "share" one with her.

Several years later, we are glad to report that many schools have changed their policies about such days and now hold more inclusive celebrations for "special people in our lives." Students are still free to bring parents, and many do, but those whose parents are working, deceased, far away, or otherwise unable to attend can instead bring another adult who is a source of strength and support in their lives. This is certainly a small adjustment—but one that can go a long way toward validating the experiences and feelings of those students who do not fit the norm.

How to Use This Information

Similarly, schools can affirm the backgrounds and current experiences of all students, and can help students to feel valued, nurtured, and accepted, by incorporating some of the following suggestions:

- Recognize that in today's schools, many students do not come from what were previously considered traditional home and family situations. Consider holding "family events" and "family information nights," rather than "parent information nights," and supporting the efforts of your "home and school association" rather than the "parent teacher association."

- Provide parents and students alike the opportunity to present their perspectives about school needs and to share their stories at special events or gatherings, so they see themselves for who they are—the most important partners in the educational venture and one of the most valuable resources available to teachers. You may consider setting a portion of the school website aside for family stories, focusing on a different student or family each month.

- Encourage students to share their own stories in a safe and nonthreatening manner. Any of the following activities may be useful, depending on your students' grade level, language proficiency, and needs:

  1. Students can each decorate a small piece of paper with an event from their own life (or from their family's history). The squares can be combined to create a quilt, a collage, or even (in a math unit) a geometric shape. Patricia Polacco's (2001) *The Keeping Quilt* is one of several books that may provide a literature-based background for this project. You may also wish to consult the Tellin' Stories project website for information about one such project, which is listed under Useful Websites.

  2. Students can complete an oral history project, interviewing each other, interviewing a family member, or (if resources permit) recording themselves telling a story. The resulting stories and experiences can be used to teach students about listening skills and interpersonal etiquette as well as the variety of experiences and cultures in the classroom.

  3. You can celebrate and value students' perseverance in the face of adversity by creating their own classroom "profile of courage." Ask each student to draw or write about a time when they faced a difficult challenge and overcame it. Students can share their experiences and then post them around the walls of the classroom. You may wish to combine this activity with readings from current events, history, or literature. (One choice for older students in history or government classes, as suggested by this activity's name, is President John F. Kennedy's book *Profiles in Courage* (2004). However, there are numerous other texts, at lower reading levels or with greater interest for younger students, that may be appropriate. Your media specialist may be able to suggest titles that are appropriate for your school's resources and your students' experiences.)

  4. Family heritage boxes, picture journals, personal timelines, and writing journals can all encourage students to chronicle their own stories in a combination of pictures and writing, using a format that may be more engaging than the typical notebook-and-pencil journal.

As always, asking students to share details about their lives calls for sensitivity and forethought. First, you may wish to time these activities so that they occur before a family information night or home-school conference, so parents, guardians, and other family members have the opportunity to see students' work. This may provide an opportunity for you to interact with family members and, also, provide a rich opportunity for students and their families to dialogue about their own experiences in an accepting, nonthreatening environment.

Second, be mindful of the information you receive from students. Acknowledge the feelings students describe and the perseverance or courage their stories highlight, without making value judgments. A few years ago, a teacher in a suburban high school was surprised to see one of her highest-performing students respond to a similar assignment by writing about how he felt when he had to travel from bar to bar looking for his mother each night, then help to carry her home and put her to bed if she was intoxicated. The teacher learned a valuable lesson that, we believe, all of us learn and relearn throughout our careers: to be mindful of the perceptions and preconceptions we have about our students (some of which may be accurate and some of which are surely not). However, the teacher also realized that she was obligated to approach the school counselor to ascertain whether this information should be reported to the county's Child Protective Services division. Whenever we ask students to share sensitive

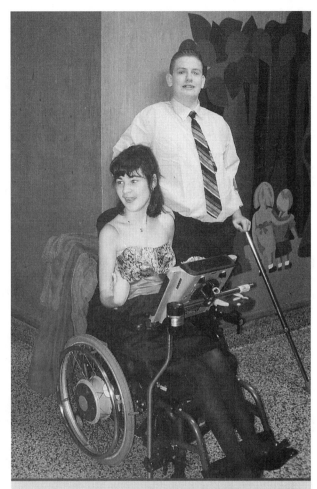

School is an important setting for the development of friendships at various levels, supporting students' social and emotional, as well as academic, growth.

topics, we need to be aware of the dual obligations of teachers: both keeping students' confidences (or respecting students' privacy), when appropriate, and knowing when it is legally or ethically incumbent to break such a confidence. Make sure that you know your county and state policies for when you are required to report students' information to others within the school—and make sure, also, that you are aware of the designated staff members with whom you should share your concerns.

4. Recognize your partners and collaborate effectively with them.

All members of the groups in Figure 5.4 are potential—and important—partners in the effort to support students' mental wellness and growth. Each may have a slightly different role to play—but each, also, possesses a slightly different set of knowledge and expertise, each of which can play an important role in the process of supporting students. Use the checklist (see Figure 5.4) to

Figure 5.4 Frequency of Communication With Others Regarding Students' Well-Being

Partner	Weekly	Monthly	Once or Twice a Year	Never
Immediate and extended family members				
School faculty and staff (ESOL, special education, specialists, general education teachers)				
Related services personnel (speech, vision, hearing personnel)				
Counselors and psychologists				
Other school staff				
Social services				
Community-based or private mental wellness services				
Community-based or private physical wellness care services				
Housing assistance agencies				
Recreation agencies or organizations				
Transportation services				
Religious or faith-based organizations				

assess how often you communicate with individuals in each of the roles regarding students' social, emotional, and physical well-being.

How to Use This Information

If you regularly collaborate with many or all of the organizations listed in Figure 5.4, you may wish to share information about them with your colleagues. If, on the other hand, you find that you are marking "once or twice a year" or "never" for many of these organizations, then we suggest that you set out to broaden your own awareness of community resources and potential mental wellness supports. Select one agency from this list each month, and spend a few hours researching the organization, gathering materials about it, or even visiting one of its offices. After you learn a bit about the agency or organization, find a way to share information about the resource with your students and their families. You might mention the agency's contact information in your class newsletter; you could post information about it on your homework website or class page; you could send a short note or list home with students. For older students, you may even share information about the resource directly with them—or, as part of a class project, have them research different organizations available within the community. Alternatively, you and your team (department, grade level, or other group) may choose to each research one of these resources and share information about them in a meeting once a semester.

SUMMARY

As the diversity of classrooms increases, teachers may be faced with students whose background, prior experiences, or current experiences are different from those they previously encountered in the classroom. As a result, teachers must make the effort to learn about students' cultural backgrounds, family situations, and experiences. In addition, teachers would be well served to become familiar with the mental health challenges that students face, ranging from the difficulty of adjusting to American school to challenges posed by family separation, socioeconomic stress, or recent moves. Collaboration and information-sharing among school professionals (within the boundaries of school and legal policies), as well as increased familiarity with community resources, can provide valuable information and tools that may be helpful to students and families.

EXTENSION AND COLLABORATION

1. Often, our efforts to connect with students and families fall into a deficit-model approach or, equally problematic, a tutorial-style pattern, where school personnel attempt to identify "problems" facing students and families and then tell them how to "fix" those issues. We encourage reverse-deficit thinking, where school staff participate in activities alongside students and

families, engage in community activities with them, and recognize that they themselves have much to learn about the richness and resiliency in students' backgrounds. The "funds of knowledge" approach, which looks at the resources in each student's background to identify sources of strength and support, is one effective model for approaching this issue (Gonzalez, Moll, & Amanti, 2005).

2. To this end, you may wish to attend a community, cultural, or even religious event with your students or their families. Check the town calendar for local festivals, discuss with your students (and their parents) what community activities or events are important to them, and attend with the goal of learning more about your students' backgrounds.

3. Many schools, recognizing the link between mental wellness and physical wellness, are taking steps to connect families with resources that relate to physical health. If your school does not have an in-school clinic or reference service, take steps to provide this information to your colleagues so that it can be shared with families throughout the school. You might ask your principal for 5 to 10 minutes to brainstorm with staff at a faculty meeting for resources and organizations that could help support families' physical wellness and nutritional needs (in addition to those that focus exclusively on mental wellness). This information could be typed on a handout and provided to families or posted on the school's website, representing the shared knowledge and investment of the school faculty.

4. Work with a small group of colleagues to create a set of minilessons focusing on resiliency, positive self-concept, and strategies for handling challenges and conflict. These should be appropriate to your students' grades and developmental levels. Keep your school schedule in mind as you develop them, so the lessons can be easily fit into classroom sessions. If you involve teachers from a variety of subjects and grade levels, it is more likely your lessons will have appeal, and be useful, across different grade levels and subjects. These minilessons can then be shared with colleagues in department, team, or whole-staff meetings.

5. As you implement activities designed to help students share their stories (discussed earlier in the chapter under New Steps to Take—Tomorrow), select one or two experiences that stand out. Share these with your colleagues in a brief announcement at a meeting, by photocopying part of your classroom activities, or by sending an e-mail to those who you know will find the information useful.

NEXT STEPS

In this chapter, you have had the opportunity to consider factors that may impact students' mental wellness. As you think about the ways in which this information is relevant to your students, you may wish to seek out resources in the community that can help you better understand your students' cultures, the stressors that may be placed on them, and resources that may help to support both your students and you. In Extension and Collaboration, which precedes this paragraph, some suggestions are made for doing so. As you move beyond this chapter into Chapter 6, you will also want to keep in mind the way that mental wellness issues can impact students' access to, and understanding of, language and curriculum. This is particularly the case with respect to academic language, where students may not be able to rely on context, body language, nonverbal communication, and prior knowledge. For this reason, it is valuable to keep an awareness of mental wellness factors in mind when thinking about language, literacy, assessments, and other topics covered in subsequent chapters in the book.

COMMUNITY CONNECTIONS

1. If your school does not currently have one, consider establishing a parent and family resource center within your school to provide mental wellness information to families of students. Even in these budget-conscious times, creative planning can help schools bring this information to families in an accessible way—without investing significant additional staff time. If a school has a dedicated family resource coordinator (or a guidance counselor who works with family members), that person may broaden the repertoire of information to include mental wellness information. If not, there are several ways to take initial steps to make such information available to parents. One school we worked with placed a small table in the school's foyer and used it to display materials and brochures (in several languages) that family members were free to take. Another set of teachers we recently worked with created a quilt to hang in the school's entrance, which listed the names and contact information for various mental wellness agencies on different panels. Next to the quilt, they displayed handouts that contained contact information from a number of the agencies.

2. Consider inviting a representative of a community agency or service organization to give a brief presentation before or after a PTA meeting. The presentation might focus on recognizing signs of mental wellness challenges, or on family strategies to build mental wellness. (Your staff members may wish to attend as well.)

3. Identify members of your community who have successfully negotiated challenges that your students may face. Consider, for example, a community college student who chose not to drop out of school; a recent immigrant who successfully acculturated to American society; or someone who overcame a challenging experience, such as war, the need to seek asylum, or similar experiences. Your local relief agency, local religious organizations, or even a local newspaper article may provide some ideas. Invite this individual to speak to your students and share their "strategies for success." If school policy allows, you may even consider inviting parents and family members to this classroom visit.

USEFUL WEBSITES

- National Association of School Psychologists: www.nasponline.org. The NASP website contains an up-to-date resource library on a variety of topics related to mental health and wellness issues, designed for both teachers and school counselors (or psychologists). Key information is provided in both Spanish and English.
- American School Counselor Association: www.schoolcounselor.org. The ASCA provides information on its website for school professionals and for parents and families, particularly in the areas of supporting students through transitions, school and home challenges, and effective collaboration between home and school.
- Center for Applied Linguistics' Funds of Knowledge Digest: www.cal .org/resources/Digest/ncrcds01.html. There are numerous organizations, articles, and books that discuss the "funds of knowledge" concept in more detail. One such reliable resource is the Center for Applied Linguistics' Digest, which provides an overview of the topic, cites relevant research, and offers strategies for implementation.
- Teaching for Change: www.teachingforchange.org/parentorg. The Teaching for Change website describes in some detail the unique Tellin' Stories project, including some useful ideas to integrate the project into curriculum and into the life of the school, as well as to ensure that a climate is created in the school that allows all members of the community to share their own stories.

6 Curriculum and Language

Making Texts and Materials Accessible

Diana knew her third-grade math students struggled, particularly those with IEPs (individualized education plans) and ESOL (English for speakers of other languages) accommodation plans, in accessing the content and completing the assignments. Acting on the advice of her department chair, she scheduled a meeting with the special education and ESOL teachers to discuss what she could change. At the meeting, she brought out her workbooks, textbook, and samples of work completed by the students whose progress concerned her most.

"It looks like they can't understand anything on the worksheet," the ESOL teacher said, looking over one student's work.

"Have you tried preteaching your vocabulary? Maybe you can give them a guide and reinforce content words after you teach them," suggested the special education teacher.

Diana sighed. She hadn't yet planned specific activities to help these students with vocabulary acquisition, but she was willing to try. Over the next two weeks, she spent her prep and even her lunch periods reviewing the textbooks, looking ahead, and making charts, graphic organizers, and word walls for the key words in each unit, words such as *quadrilateral* and *pentagon*. Each day, she charted how a few specific students did on their worksheets. Much to her dismay, she saw little progress.

Finally, she asked one of her students, Josue, point-blank: "Josue, point to the words you don't understand."

She was shocked to see him point to the first, third, and fifth words in the directions: "Underline the correct word beneath each shape."

"He didn't even get to the content vocabulary!" Diana exclaimed to the ESOL teacher a little later. "I spent all that time preteaching *quadrilateral,* and he doesn't even know what *underline* means. I had no idea what he really needed to know." She looked up at her colleague, frustrated. "So what do I do now?"

THE ISSUES

- Students' ability to access the "language of instruction"
- Teacher preconceptions about what language is most challenging for students
- Accessibility of textbooks and materials for diverse learners
- BICS (basic interpersonal communicative skills) versus CALP (cognitive academic language proficiency)
- Need for greater "sheltering" of instructional materials, assessments, and teacher language (see Figure 6.8 on page 93 for an explanation of sheltering)

QUESTIONS TO CONSIDER

1. How did Diana attempt to determine her students' level of language proficiency? What techniques were (or were not) successful?

2. How quickly can Josue and other students be expected to acquire the academic language needed for classroom success?

3. How does the timeline for language acquisition impact instruction?

4. What obligations does Diana have to Josue and her other students who struggle with the language demands (as opposed to content) of her lessons?

5. What could Diana feasibly do in order to make her textbooks, worksheets, activities, and assessments accessible to Josue? How could her colleagues in ESOL and other departments support her in doing so?

GETTING THE ANSWERS

For many teachers, one of the challenges of a highly diverse classroom is the need to deliver standards-based instruction, within a specific curriculum and geared toward specific assessments, to students who may have little or no English proficiency. Language acquisition is a lengthy process, and students who may appear to be fluent when they speak with friends at the lunch table may actually have a much harder time mastering academic English within a classroom setting (Cummins, 2007). In Chapter 1, linguist Jim Cummins describes this phenomenon by drawing a distinction between BICS (basic interpersonal communication skills) and CALP (cognitive academic language proficiency). BICS refers to the use of everyday language—what some teachers call playground English or lunchroom English. Phrases such as "Where is the bathroom?" or "I'd like the pizza" draw on basic interpersonal language skills—they involve use of language common to everyday functioning, rather than demanding higher-level, academic vocabulary. BICS also are content saturated—if a student lacks the language proficiency to pronounce or use the word *pizza* correctly, it is likely the individual can supplement the words by pointing to the pizza, picking up the pizza, or smiling and nodding when someone else offers the pizza. Cummins (2007) theorizes that most culturally and linguistically diverse (CLD) students acquire BICS in one to three years.

CALP, on the other hand, refers to the use of academic language, which is usually more advanced *and* not as clearly linked to context. Phrases such as "Identify the factors that led to the start of the Civil War" are considered to make heavy use of academic vocabulary—the content-specific term *Civil War,* as well as the more challenging terms, *identify, factors,* and perhaps even *start,* are all terms that a student might not learn from everyday experience. Unlike BICS, CALP cannot generally be communicated through nonverbal, paraverbal, or context clues. See Figure 6.1 for further explanation. (Unlike the pizza example, there is no "factor"

Body language and gestures are two examples of nonverbal elements that are nonetheless important elements of language.

nearby to which a teacher can gesture while a student attempts to answer that question.) And CALP is not fully acquired for five to seven years, or even longer.

In addition to understanding the demands of academic language, as opposed to basic, everyday language, it is important to know the stages of second-language acquisition. How long should it take Josue to understand what Diana is saying? What should his process of language acquisition "look" like?

Figure 6.1 Language Context in the Classroom

Nonverbal clues: Nonverbal communication involves communication without using words: gestures, body language, facial expression, and movement.

Nonverbal communication in the classroom: A teacher asks Maritza to come to the front of the room. When Maritza hesitates, the teacher gestures to her. Maritza comes to the front of the room.

Paraverbal clues: Paraverbal communication involves communication through the *way* in which one uses words: tone, volume, emphasis, and pitch.

Paraverbal communication in the classroom: The teacher asks students to turn to Page 17. Steven turns to Page 7. The teacher repeats the direction, raising her voice slightly on the word *seventeen* and pronouncing it more slowly: "Turn to page *seventeen.*" Steven turns to the correct page.

The diagram in Figure 6.2 illustrates the commonly accepted stages of the process that are typical for most students who are learning a second language.

Based on the limited information in the case study that began this chapter, where would you place Josue along this continuum?

Figure 6.2 Stages of Second-Language Acquisition

Silent or Preproduction Stage (Student is silent much of the time, learning language receptively without necessarily expressing himself or herself orally.)

↓

Early Production Stage (Student may be beginning to use words, pronounce English sounds, and communicate with peers or teachers.)

↓

Speech Emergence Stage (Student is beginning to use everyday, basic language more consistently and with greater complexity.)

↓

Intermediate Language Proficiency Stage (Student is using some academic language, including specialized content vocabulary and key words, with increasing accuracy.)

↓

Advanced Language Proficiency Stage (Student speaks fluently and with accuracy.)

Consider your own classroom and students. At what stage do most of *your* ELL students appear to be? Take a moment to complete the chart in Figure 6.3; you may see some similarities to your own students.

Figure 6.3	How Does Second-Language Acquisition "Look" in the Classroom?

In order to apply the knowledge you just gained regarding second-language acquisition, take a moment to match each of these descriptions to the appropriate stage of second-language acquisition:

Stages

A. Preproduction

B. Early Production

C. Speech Emergence

D. Intermediate Language Proficiency

E. Advanced Language Proficiency

1. _____Esteban has been in the United States for about a year. He still speaks in Spanish when with his friends, and his ESOL teacher reports that he relies heavily upon Spanish when completing work in her class. Esteban is beginning to use English words and has recently begun attempting to initiate communication with his teachers using sentences spoken only in English.

2. _____Ricardo arrived in the United States about four months ago. He occasionally speaks to peers in his native language but does not speak at all to his teachers. He appears shy but friendly (he smiles frequently and uses nonverbal communication effectively to request items in the cafeteria, in PE class, and even in some of his academic classes).

3. _____Obafemi has been in the United States for about five years. He was recently exited from ESOL services after successfully completing the highest level of the ESOL curriculum. Obafemi participates in all general education content classes. He is an active participant in class discussions, raising his hand and using fairly complex sentences. He reads and writes without needing day-to-day support from the classroom teacher. While his writing still occasionally contains grammatical errors, he is able to correct them quickly and accurately if his attention is brought to them.

4. _____Elena has been in the United States for three years and has recently been moved to mainstream content classes. She still attends ESOL classes as well but has been moved to the second-highest level of ESOL offered by the school. Elena can complete the reading and most assignments in her content classes successfully, though she still uses a dictionary frequently, reads and writes much more slowly than her peers, and occasionally has questions about vocabulary and sentence structure when she reads independently.

5. _____Maria has been in the United States for about two years. She has recently been placed in sheltered math, science, and social studies classes, where she receives extra support with vocabulary, reading, and writing. Maria is able to write complete sentences in English and communicates with her teachers effectively to share most of her wants and needs ("I would like to use the bathroom," "When is this assignment due?").

Answers: 1: B. 2: A. 3: E. 4: D. 5: C.

NEW STEPS TO TAKE—TOMORROW

1. Identify the language demands of your classroom and curriculum.

In applying these principles to practice, you may want to start by thinking about your own use of classroom language. Take a moment to identify examples of BICS and CALP from your own classroom instruction and content area. (You may wish to consult Figure 6.6 on identifying academic vocabulary.) When you identify CALP (academic language), remember to include idiomatic language too, as students frequently need a specialized frame of reference, or significant experience with English, to understand that, for example, "Take time to smell the roses" means "Take time to enjoy the finer things in life." If possible, think of the lesson you taught today (or will teach tomorrow) in filling out the chart in Figure 6.4 (BICS and CALP in My Classroom).

Now, identify the support that is available in your class, instruction, and content area for students who may struggle with CALP (Figure 6.5).

Finally, identify the types of additional support that would be useful for your students in mastering academic language. You may wish to consult with a colleague (a member of your team, an ESOL teacher, or a special educator) in generating ideas to note in Figure 6.7.

How to Use This Information

As you complete this chart, take some time to think, also, about the most likely sources of this support. Often, classroom teachers feel the burden for accommodating students' linguistic needs and adapting the curriculum to meet those needs falls disproportionately on their shoulders. You may find that support is available in unexpected places. Your school's ESOL teacher or foreign language teacher may be able to offer help with specific vocabulary. If a student has a sibling or close friend whose language proficiency is more advanced, that person may be able to offer the student some support. Even if you do not have direct knowledge of a student's first language and, therefore, can't translate specific words or phrases, you may be surprised at the difference that it makes when you shelter your language (see Figure 6.8 for suggestions on sheltering instruction for ELLs).

2. Consider how the process of second-language acquisition might impact your students and your instruction.

Each school district, or school, has different policies on the point at which students are included in the general education setting. Some teachers may encounter students at the very beginning stages of language proficiency, especially those who teach subjects such as physical education, art, or music. Others may not see ELL students until they reach the later stages of the second-language acquisition process.

Figure 6.4 BICS and CALP in My Classroom

Basic, Everyday Words I Use in My Classroom (BICS)	Academic, Content-Specific Language My Students Need to Know (CALP)

Figure 6.5 Support Already Present in My Class for Students Learning CALP

What support is already present for my students as they identify and master academic language?
(Examples might include the following: The textbook highlights vocabulary; the teacher reinforces vocabulary; or leveled textbooks or worksheets are available.)

Figure 6.6 Identifying Academic Vocabulary in Your Content Area and Grade Level

One of the most common questions teachers ask is, "How do I know what is 'BICS' and what is 'CALP,' or academic language?" It's a good question—and a complex one. Like any complex question, it does not have one single "right" answer. The language demands of a kindergarten classroom are very different from those of a sixth-grade or twelfth-grade classroom; and for that reason, it is not possible to provide a list of words that, always and everywhere, will represent the sum total of academic language. There are such lists—and you can easily find them by doing an Internet search for "academic language." These lists may be one helpful tool in the process of identifying academic words, but they are certainly not the only one. We suggest that you use a multistep process to identify words that might be common academic language in your classroom.

Creating an Academic Language List

1. Review your curriculum and highlight important content vocabulary that students must master.

2. Review directions commonly given on your assignments and assessments. Highlight any words that would not appear in the context of typical everyday conversation for a child of that grade level.

3. Add to the list prepositions, conjunctions (particularly those that are less commonly used), numbers (especially larger numbers), colors, days of the week and the month, and other common words. (Some of these may be most relevant to the elementary classroom, where colors and days represent content knowledge as well as background knowledge.)

4. Consider other social and cultural information, including terms and concepts, that students need to know in your classroom. Many native English speakers have at least heard of the Civil War—but a student new to the United States might have a very different war in mind from that of 1861 to 1865!

5. Review your materials (and your own speech and language use) for idiomatic language. Do you use phrases that have a different meaning from the denotative definition of the words they include? For example, "a drop in the bucket," "add fuel to the fire," and "15 minutes of fame" are all commonly accepted phrases in English, and many (though not all) native speakers would likely understand, at least partially, the meaning and intent of such a phrase. However, for non-native speakers, that task becomes considerably more difficult (a student reading the phrase "add fuel to the fire" could reasonably be expected to ask, "But where's the fire? There's nothing in the reading about a fire!")

6. Finally, ask a colleague who teaches the same grade and content area to review your list and suggest anything that seems to be missing.

Therefore, the chart in Figure 6.9 is one that you will want to use in a way that makes sense according to your own school policy and your own student population. For example, if you tend to have students at the later stages of language proficiency in your own classroom, focus your time on the bottom sections of the chart.

Use the chart in Figure 6.9 to identify what elements of your classroom currently *are*—and *are not*—accessible to students at various stages of second-language acquisition. Think back to the Chapter 1 discussion of student "can-ness," where the spotlight is on the abilities and talents that do exist rather than those that appear to be missing: We want to use models built on existing strengths and potential benefits (not on deficits). For that reason, this chart helps to frame your analysis in terms of what your students already can do and understand, rather than focusing on what they cannot do. Consider the ways in which your classroom already is accessible, and use that knowledge to plan for continued instruction that is responsive to their needs.

| Figure 6.7 | Additional Support for Students in Mastering Academic Language |

What additional support would be helpful for my students in mastering the academic language demands of my classroom?

(Examples might include preteaching specific vocabulary; creating word walls with definitions or pictures alongside to help students access the meaning; providing example problems on worksheets or assessments to help students understand the directions; increasing one-on-one support from the teacher during individual work time; and highlighting and reviewing academic words on take-home activities.)

| Figure 6.8 | Sheltering Classroom Instruction for ELLs |

Sheltering is a term applied to instruction where content is delivered in English, but the teacher takes extra steps to make sure the language is accessible to diverse learners. Sheltered English can also be known as SDAIE (specially designed academic instruction in English), SIOP (sheltered instruction and observation protocol), or SEI (structured English immersion) (Parker, 1985; Broekhuizen, 2004; NCELA, 2006).

Following are some suggestions for sheltering your content if you are not able to provide students with native-language support in your classroom:

- Include extra "wait time" by pausing after sentences, key words, or directions. This allows students time to process what you have said.
- Reinforce vocabulary and directions with visual aids.
- As much as possible, standardize directions (use the same directions whenever possible, and teach the key words in each direction); so students can understand, can gain skill and experience over time, and become familiar with your classroom routines.
- Simplify sentence structures. For example, you might plan to say something like "After lunch, everybody should come in and sit down, unless you have already completed your math problems, and then you can have an extra five minutes of recess." To make this sentence more accessible to your students, consider breaking it down into shorter sentences: "If you still need to do math, come back after lunch. If you are done with math, you may stay outside." (As this is still a complex concept, you could also supplement your oral directions with a note on the board.)

Figure 6.9 Second-Language Acquisition Process

Stage of Language Acquisition	What are students able to do at this level?	What might be challenging for students at this level?	What elements of my instruction currently make use of students' strengths?	What elements could I add or improve to support students at this stage?
Preproduction (model)	My students at this stage can listen and can understand some spoken language. They can also, with time and scaffolding, understand some written language.	Expressive language: talking and writing on their own	I make sure that I shelter my language, so I know they can at least understand key words. I also pair them with peers, so they have opportunities to be exposed to student language as well as teacher language.	I can incorporate more visuals into my instruction, so students can learn from the pictures even if they do not understand all the words. I can also give them varied opportunities to produce language, so it will be easier for them when they are ready.
Preproduction				
Early production				
Speech emergence				
Intermediate language proficiency				
Advanced language proficiency				

How to Use This Information

This chart (Figure 6.9) may be only partially relevant to your student population and your classroom. For example, if you teach an AP (advanced placement) high school physics class, it is unlikely you would have any students at the preproduction stage of language acquisition. For that reason, consider it (like most things in this book) as a guide and organizer rather than a rigid pattern to follow in sequence. Complete the rows that you see as being most relevant to your students—the ones you have now, the ones you have had in the past, or the ones you may have in a future teaching assignment.

As with most sections of this book, the entries on this chart may also be most useful when shared. Take the time to discuss your answers with a colleague—both to benefit from one another's knowledge and to widen your horizons—perhaps you do not teach any students at the preproduction phase, but your colleague very well may.

3. Become familiar with the elements of language and their implications for classroom instruction.

How to Use This Information

When considering the impact of each of these elements of language on your students (see Figure 6.10), you will want to think about your students' age, developmental level, prior experiences with language and literacy, and cultural framework. You will also want to think about how you, as a teacher, view your students' language and, indirectly or directly, teach language. Do you focus on reducing their "syntactic ambiguities," asking them to repeat words or phrases that may seem unclear? Do you prioritize pragmatics, modeling appropriate interactions, teaching behaviors or appropriate phrases, and providing time to talk about how classroom communication is going? Your own approach has the potential to impact how your students' language develops and what they remember as important about language.

After thinking about these elements of language, use the chart in Figure 6.11 to note your responses. For this chart, we are not providing specific directions—rather, for each element of language, consider your students' chronological, developmental,

Access to different language-rich, developmentally appropriate experiences can build students' language proficiency as well as their social and cultural knowledge and skills.

Figure 6.10	Linguistic Complexity and Elements of Language

Element of Language and Definition	Classroom Relevance
Phonetics and phonology: Have to do with the sounds of language—how students produce sounds and put them together, and how the sounds correspond to symbols in the English alphabet.	Students' articulation of words and phrases may be impacted by differences between their native language and English. For example, native Spanish speakers may find that certain sounds in English are difficult to pronounce, as they do not exist in Spanish (English *j*, for example). These differences are not the result of language delay or disability but, rather, of linguistic diversity. Derwing (2003) discusses the way in which nonnative English speakers perceive their accents and the way in which students' perception of their own speech can impact self-esteem and the acculturation process.
Morphology: Has to do with the way in which morphemes—the smallest possible units of meaning—in language are arranged to create words and meaning (for example, the word *walked* contains two morphemes, one for *walk* and one for *ed*).	As students progress through the stages of language acquisition (in either a first language, known as L1, or a second language, known as L2), they become more familiar with the structures by which words are created. Students who are still learning formal language—in L1 or L2—may need additional support in correctly attaching prefixes, suffixes, and grammatical markers (such as *ed* to identify past tense, or *s* to indicate a plural).
Syntax: Has to do with the arrangement of words into sentences to create meaning. Also has to do with the idea of grammaticality—for example, what is grammatical according to standard English, and what is not? Linguistic theory states that all languages and dialects are inherently grammatical—that is, they all have rules and structures that govern conventions and usage. Even dialects and languages that are considered to be nonstandard (or not typically used in the classroom) are still grammatical in this sense.	English, despite being confusing and complex in many respects, has a fairly consistent rule regarding word order. Sentences most often occur in the pattern of subject-verb-direct object. As might be expected, second-language learners who are used to different patterns may find this confusing and may need time and additional support to correctly use English grammatical rules. With regard to syntax, as well as other branches of language, it is also important to keep in mind the distinction between a "prescriptive" approach to grammar (in which one makes judgments characterizing usage as correct or incorrect) and a "descriptive" one (in which one describes a student's language, without making a value judgment about right or wrong speech, and identifies support that would be useful to the student in acquiring full English proficiency).
Semantics: Has to do with the construction of meaning, the way in which words refer to concepts or constructs, and the meaning of words and phrases.	Students may need additional support in using the correct word, identifying shades of meaning, and understanding idiomatic language. Preview your assignment, instructional materials, and assessments to identify words or phrases that may be confusing to students.
Pragmatics: Has to do with the social conventions surrounding language use. Turn-taking, speech patterns, social interactions, use of appropriate conventions, and even nonverbal or paraverbal elements are part of pragmatics.	For students from other cultures, the social conventions surrounding communication may be as new and unfamiliar as the linguistic elements of language. Practices such as eye contact, hand gestures, vocal tone and volume, and interaction with adults and peers are not universal—rather, they are culturally mediated (Vygotsky, 1978) and are not learned instantly (or intuitively) when students enter a new culture.

Figure 6.11 Elements of Language and Potential Relevance for Classroom Instruction

Element of Language	Potential Relevance for Classroom Instruction
Phonetics and phonology	Hmmm . . . I notice my Spanish-speaking third-grade students often have trouble with *z* and *j* sounds. I think it must be because those sounds don't exist, or exist differently, in the Spanish language. Maybe I can find ways to explicitly model those sounds—or work with the SLP [speech language pathologist] on staff to get some suggestions. In the meantime, what about their spelling tests and the listening portion of their achievement tests? I bet if they have a hard time speaking those sounds, it is hard to process and write the words that use those sounds. I'll bring that up at our next team meeting. Maybe we can give them some targeted instruction prior to tests—or differentiate the grading for these students, at least on informal assessments.

Element of Language	Potential Relevance for Classroom Instruction
Phonetics and phonology	
Morphology	
Syntax	
Semantics	
Pragmatics	

Students can benefit from additional feedback and support in a one-on-one setting to further support the development of academic language skills.

emotional, academic, cultural, and linguistic backgrounds and needs. Then, use the space to write down your observations about the way in which that particular category of language might be relevant—both in terms of your students' performance and your own instruction. You may choose to think of this as a sort of journal and structure your responses accordingly, so you can think through the issues that may exist with your students.

Once you have jotted your thoughts down, review them and identify changes you may want to make—or next steps you may want to take—based on what you've indicated. Consider sharing your ideas with colleagues; some suggestions for doing so follow (see Extension and Collaboration, and Next Steps).

SUMMARY

As we've discussed, considering the topic of language in a classroom involves much more than simply highlighting content-area vocabulary. A student's linguistic, educational, social, physical, cognitive, and cultural background all have roles in impacting the student's language production. To identify the language demands of your classroom, consider each of these in relationship to your own curriculum and teaching style. By doing so, you can isolate academic vocabulary that may be particularly challenging for your students and can identify steps that may make mastery of that vocabulary easier.

EXTENSION AND COLLABORATION

This chapter addresses only a few of the factors that can impact—and be impacted by—a student's use of language. You may want to spend some time thinking about these factors and deepening your knowledge in this area.

1. Search the Internet for "linguistic performance" and "linguistic competence," two concepts popularized by the work of linguist Noam Chomsky. Spend some time considering the way in which a student's competence, or knowledge, might differ from the student's actual performance, and what factors might account for this difference.

2. Review your entries on the chart regarding second-language acquisition earlier in this chapter (see Figure 6.9). Select the phase of second-language acquisition that you find most applicable to the student population in your

school (for example, your school may have a large number of newly arrived students in the beginning phases). Take a few minutes to share the strategies or suggestions in your chart with your colleagues—at a staff meeting, team meeting, or informal get-together.

3. Think about what you have learned about language in this chapter and in your discussions with colleagues. Using that information, review your school's most recent parent or family newsletter or bulletin. Identify words or phrases that may be challenging for parents who are themselves English language learners, and suggest modifications. Present your findings at the next staff meeting or on the school's staff website.

NEXT STEPS

Language is key, not only to social and emotional interactions with students but also as a diagnostic indicator. Awareness of a student's language-use patterns can provide valuable information about the student's needs—linguistic, academic, and etiological. For this reason, it is particularly important to be sensitive to the variety of factors that can impact CLD students' language production in the classroom—during all phases of second-language acquisition. The remaining chapters in this book continue to address these factors, considering the relationship between language and culture in the assessment process, developing literacy skills, addressing students' mental and emotional wellness, and connecting with families to form productive home-school partnerships.

COMMUNITY CONNECTIONS

1. Building on your work in Number 3 (listed in the preceding paragraphs under Extension and Collaboration), consider reviewing all of your school's parent and family outreach efforts with an eye toward linguistic accessibility. You may work on updating the school's website to be more linguistically accessible, for example, or creating a dictionary of "school terms" for parents and family members new to the school.

2. Have your students become lexicographers (dictionary makers) themselves. Students can "collect" words in their homes and communities that relate to your subject or content area, and can create their own lists or books of important words. This may help students establish personal connections to your subject area—while allowing you some insight into their lives and backgrounds.

3. There are numerous organizations that volunteer to teach English to adults. Consider volunteering for one—or at least visiting to find out more about the resources available to English language learner adults in your community. You may be able to provide some of this information to parents and family members of your students.

USEFUL WEBSITES

- Center for Applied Linguistics: www.cal.org. The Center for Applied Linguistics has a wealth of resources regarding linguistics on its website. You can research key areas of theory, policy, and practice relating to language.
- Dr. Cummins's ESL and Second Language Learning: www.iteachilearn.com/cummins. Dr. Jim Cummins, a noted linguist, has an exceptionally informative website that covers topics of language and literacy, as well as discusses classroom applications of each.
- Stephen D. Krashen: www.sdkrashen.com. Dr. Stephen Krashen's five hypotheses of second-language acquisition, though not covered in this chapter, are extremely useful in helping teachers to understand the process and socioemotional context of second-language acquisition. Dr. Krashen's website contains links to articles and commentaries describing the hypotheses in further detail.

7 Literacy Development

Factors Impacting Diverse Learners

Raoul, a first-year computer science teacher at Cordova Springs High School, felt himself to be once again confused. Everywhere he looked, he encountered a different definition of literacy. His principal had exhorted everyone to focus on reading strategies so that the students would be successful on their state reading and literacy exams. Meanwhile, the computer science textbook that he used for his ninth-grade class devoted an entire chapter to computer literacy—and he thought the activities had nothing to do with reading skills. As he contemplated the difference between the two, he heard in the back of his mind a phrase his college reading professor had frequently used: "Literacy is more about the development of the child than about the development of the child's skills."

"So which is the right definition?" Raoul wondered. "If I want to really support my students' literacy development, what does that mean I have to do? And if my students are all in high school, why do I have to be worried about their literacy anyway? They all should have learned to read long ago."

THE ISSUES

- Definitions and stages of *literacy*
- Impact of second-language acquisition on literacy
- Scaffolding literacy goals for students with exceptionalities
- Culturally responsive literacy practices and assessment

QUESTIONS TO CONSIDER

1. How might Raoul begin to sort through the differing definitions of literacy? Which definition or approach toward literacy is appropriate for his classroom practice and for his students?

2. How is literacy development relevant to students from K–12 and beyond, and what does literacy mean beyond "just" decoding skills?

3. How does the process of second-language acquisition impact literacy?

4. How can Raoul support literacy development for his students along the continuum of needs, including those who are second-language learners as well as those who are not?

GETTING THE ANSWERS

Literacy, as Raoul noticed in the vignette above, is a term used to refer to several different concepts. Literacy is often understood to be the ability to decode words and match sounds with alphabet letters in order to accomplish basic reading and writing skills (Central Intelligence Agency, 2009). This definition, used in surveys by the Census Bureau and numerous other organizations that compute "literacy rates," is simple: "the ability to read and write by a specified age" (commonly an age in adolescence or early adulthood, such as 15) (Central Intelligence Agency, 2009, para. 1). Some theorists take a more holistic view of literacy, linking it to proficiency in language and communication in general, rather than reading and writing alone. The National Institute for Literacy (2009) uses a definition that draws on this view, taken from the Federal Workforce Investment Act of 1998: Literacy is "an individual's ability to read, write, and speak in English, compute, and solve problems, at levels of proficiency necessary to function on the job, in the family of the individual, and in society" (para. 1). Literacy is also frequently associated with the ability to make meaning out of a set of knowledge or experiences or to negotiate a complex system of rules and information (such as computer literacy, tech literacy, and social literacy) (United Nations Educational, Scientific and Cultural Organization [UNESCO], 2004).

We subscribe to a "both-and" view of literacy. We do acknowledge the importance of decoding skills, reading comprehension, and writing skills as a key element of an individual's literacy. However, we also embrace the idea that oral communication is as relevant in literacy development and literacy instruction as written communication is, and an inclusive definition of literacy involves all four components of language use (reading, writing, listening, and speaking) (International Reading Association, 2009). We further believe that literacy can be understood to refer to an individual's ability to navigate through our complex system of social, economic, cultural, and linguistic expectations in order to reach a desired goal (UNESCO, 2004). In our view, one corollary to this belief is that an individual may possess well-developed literacy skills, in this sense, without being a fully proficient reader and writer. While the goal of literacy instruction may still be to help a child become a proficient reader, writer, listener, and speaker; we firmly believe that such instruction must begin with the recognition that the child already possesses the ability to make complex meaning from language—even if he or she does not have the skills to apply that knowledge to print—and that literacy instruction must begin by recognizing

Reading together can be a valuable way for students to build literacy skills and learn from one another.

the child's strengths rather than proceeding from a deficit-oriented focus on the lack of print-language skills.

This debate is not new to the educational world; it is frequently discussed within the context of the whole-language, phonics-based, and blended approaches (Kuder & Hasit, 2002).

And we are well aware that the majority of schools and school systems consider literacy to be primarily relevant to reading and writing skills—in large part due, perhaps, to the increasing demands of standardized reading assessments that purport to measure a child's degree of literacy and to the federal government's own emphasis on research-based reading interventions that are expected to address topics such as alphabetic and phonemic awareness and fluency with print (Institute of Education Sciences, 2007; National Reading Panel, 2000). Acknowledging this framework, we nevertheless believe that, particularly with CLD students, a broader definition of literacy is the most appropriate. Such an outlook provides a way to appropriately identify, support, and assess those students whose written language may be below grade level (due to acculturation, second-language acquisition, trauma, disability, or other factors) but who demonstrate other skills in areas that are traditionally of lower priority in the educational system. These students may be accomplished in their oral language, in their social skills and ability to adapt, in their resiliency in the face of challenging situations, in their ability to shoulder adult responsibility, and in numerous other areas. Using a traditional definition of literacy, these students might well be labeled "deficient" in their skills. However, this designation would ignore the richness of experience, background, and ability that these students bring to the classroom setting, which can serve as building blocks for further language and literacy development (Elley & Mangubhai, 1983; Moll, 1994). Some scholars, in fact, advocate for a view of literacy that encompasses students' proficiency in navigating complex technology and media, arguing that these skills are at least as important to long-term success as the ability to read the printed word (Thoman & Jolls, 2004). For this reason, we subscribe to a definition of literacy that emphasizes the four language arts: reading, writing, listening, and speaking, rather than just the first two (Peregoy & Boyle, 2008).

How does richness of background impact literacy skills?

At this point, you may be saying to yourself, "That's well and good, but I don't see how students' backgrounds—their diverse cultural, linguistic, familial, social, or socioeconomic experiences—can really, empirically help them to be better readers, writers, speakers, users of the written word, and critical thinkers. That sounds like pie-in-the-sky theory rather than sound and practical guidance for the classroom!" There are numerous researchers and practitioners who have supported the idea that increased oral-language competency, as well as print-language instruction, can indirectly or directly support the acquisition of literacy skills, particularly for culturally and linguistically diverse (CLD) students (Peregoy & Boyle, 2008; Páez, Tabors, & López, 2007; Thomas & Collier, 2002; Genesee, Lindholm-Leary, Saunders, & Christian, 2006; August & Shanahan, 2006). According to the "interactive" model of reading (which has some similarity to the "balanced approach" method of combining whole-language and phonics-based instruction), the process of reading involves a synthesis of the student's own background and experience with the printed text on the page (Rumelhart, 2004).

Given this fact, the process of evaluating a student's literacy requires taking stock of the unique strengths, skills, and experiences that the student brings to encounters with text. Existing perceptions and knowledge impact the way in which the student constructs meaning from the text. While this situation will unfold differently for each student, of each background, you may wish to keep the following in mind when considering factors that impact a student's literacy. The list in Figure 7.1 should not be taken as a litany of potential deficits—research shows that many of these factors, such as proficiency in a language other than English, can have a positive impact on a student's literacy development.

Each of these factors (see Figure 7.1) can impact the development of literacy skills and, also, the ability to complete literacy tasks such as reading, identifying the main idea, writing, and summarizing.

Because it is difficult to assign absolute value to a student's status at any point of development, educators often use a continuum of terms to denote the gradual acquisition of those skills. This is known as the "emergent literacy"

Figure 7.1 Factors That May Play a Role in a Student's Literacy Development

Factor	Questions for Teachers to Ask
Native-language proficiency	What is the student's native language? Is the child proficient in that language?
Additional language proficiency	What is the student's additional language, or languages? How proficient is the student in additional languages?
Process of second-language acquisition	If the student is in the process of acquiring a second language, what stage is the individual in? How might the characteristics of this stage (listed in the preceding chapter) impact literacy development and reading performance?
Family status	Is there separation among family members? Does this impact the child's access to reading and literacy outside the school setting?
Prior schooling	What prior educational experiences did the child have? Has the child had interrupted educational experiences? Did the child have prior exposure to literacy? Were books and printed materials readily available in the prior school setting?
Social and socioeconomic status	What is the child's current social and socioeconomic status? What was the child's previous socioeconomic status? Has the child's status in this regard ever impacted—positively or negatively—access to printed materials or books?
Etiological factors and disabilities	Are there any disabilities present? Has the child been identified for special education services? How do these abilities impact the child's access to literacy or ability to complete literacy-related tasks? Sometimes a child with a disability may also present with corresponding strengths—well-developed oral comprehension that may compensate for a visual-processing difficulty, for example.
Degree of acculturation	To what degree has the child had the opportunity to become acculturated? Is the student's acculturation status impacting access to literacy or ability to complete literacy-related tasks? (Some reading tasks are culturally bound: "Find the main idea," for example.) Not every culture assigns equal importance to the main idea; not every cultural or linguistic group identifies the main idea as the most important element of text.

model, and suggests that the acquisition of reading skills is a lengthy process that spans the years before *and* after a child first learns to read. The stages in this process are described in the following paragraphs:

Emergent Literacy

Overview. The emergent literacy phase is one in which students begin to make sense of the world of print (Peregoy & Boyle, 2008; Clay, 1979; Kuder & Hasit, 2002). Typically, this phase occurs when students are very young, in or before preschool years. Some researchers (Clay, 1979) consider this phase to begin at birth. The emergent literacy phase involves increased awareness of print, growing understanding of the concept of directionality (i.e., writing in

English goes from left to right), and meaningful interaction with literature and language. Listening to oral or read-aloud stories, drawing pictures of characters, discussing stories, writing pretend letters, telling one's own stories, and listening to and understanding directions are all indicators of a child's progress through the emergent literacy phase. A child in this stage may pick up a book and "read" it to himself or a caregiver (telling the story in his own words rather than using that which is on the printed page), or may write her parent a note using pictures or scribbles. Each of these behaviors is appropriate for an emergent reader.

Relevance for Diverse Learners. In the emergent literacy phase, culture is as important as language in its impact on the way students construct their own literacy experiences and use language. There may be social norms that influence the way a child listens or tells a story; there may be cultural content in a story that a teacher may not understand or may find atypical. A child who is also in the process of acquiring a second language may find it easier to develop literacy skills in the first language rather than the second. The child should be encouraged to do so; research has shown that literacy skills developed in the first language transfer over to the second (August & Shanahan, 2006; Cummins, 2007; Thomas & Collier, 2002). For students who have an actual disability (as opposed to those who are in the processes of second-language acquisition or acculturation), it is equally important to provide rich literacy experiences. For children with visual impairments, for example, the presence of literacy-based activities helps to support language as well as literacy development (Day, McDonnell, & Heathfield, 2005). The emergent literacy model posits that students have a rich command of language and communication skills even before they begin to decode print and that this repertoire of communication and cognitive skills must be developed. This holds true for children who are not developing typically, as well as those who are. While students may acquire the ability to read print at different stages, family members and teachers can and should work to provide them with an appropriate range of rich and meaningful literacy experiences, including oral language as well as print (Purcell-Gates, 1996; Sulzby & Teale, 1991; Lopez-Reina, 1996; Perry, 1997).

Developing or Early Literacy

Overview. Developing, or early, readers are beginning to decode words and attach meaning to sounds and symbols (Kuder & Hasit, 2002; Johnson & Sulzby, 1999). Students who are at the developing, or developmental, stage may be able to read simple sentences and even short, simple books. They may also sound words out using invented spelling that omits letters or uses combinations of words and letters that do not appear in the correctly spelled word (for example, writing *going* as *goeg*, *friend* as *frend*, or *hippopotamus* as *hpptamis*). Developing readers continue to build upon their cognitive and communication skills as well as their awareness of print conventions and their phonetic awareness. Therefore, activities for developing readers should continue to provide a wide variety of ways to interact with the material they read, to produce and "publish" their own writing, and to explore their own perceptions of the meaning of the texts they read. Activities such as writing stories and plays, discussing stories in various ways, and listening to poetry and songs (and creating their own) can all scaffold the development of literacy skills in this stage. As students continue to become more aware of print and spelling conventions, it is suggested that teachers focus on encouraging students' production of language—in other words, encouraging them to write down their story as it occurs to them and to worry about the correct spelling only after they have gotten their ideas down on paper (Johnson & Sulzby, 1999; International Reading Association & National Association for the Education of Young Children, 1998).

Relevance for Diverse Learners. As with emergent literacy, the developmental stage of literacy is one in which students' diverse cultural and linguistic experiences, including the process of second-language acquisition, must be taken into account. Particularly as students develop phonemic awareness, those who are second-language learners may demonstrate atypical pronunciation of some sounds that exist in the English language (such as *j*, or jay; and *x*, or ex; which do not exist in a number of languages) and may have difficulty recalling the English spelling for words that include those sounds, as they may not be found in the student's native language, the one with which the individual is most familiar. Prior literacy or schooling experiences may also play a role in the speed with which a child approaches or progresses through the developmental literacy phase: The student may be mastering the norms of American school and, at the same time, may be working on the conventions of reading and writing. Finally, students who have disabilities should continue to enjoy rich literacy experiences, with

appropriate modifications or accommodations that allow them to access the language (oral and written) used in their classroom and home. These might include visual aids to enhance receptive language (writing and listening) or augmentative communication boards to support students' expressive language (via a picture board with a support person to write ideas down, or using a computer or voice synthesizer to generate a written or auditory response).

For secondary students, literacy instruction can involve working with peers or teachers on authentic reading and writing activities involving materials such as job applications, resumes, and career-related brochures.

Intermediate Literacy

Overview. In the intermediate phase of literacy development, students continue to develop as readers, writers, listeners, and speakers. Having increased their fluency and their production of language, students can now focus on mastering the conventions associated with language use: more accurate spelling, adherence to the rules of grammar, expectations of various forms of oral and written communication (for example, how is the format of a letter different from a shopping list? How is a formal speech different from the conversation you might have with your friends?) (Kuder & Hasit, 2002). Keep in mind, also, that students in the intermediate stage of literacy acquisition are just that—intermediate. The expectations placed on these students should reflect that reality, as this stage is different (and the repertoire of skills that students possess is different) from that of advanced literacy. Continued development of literacy skills in this phase can include activities that help students consciously activate their prior knowledge ("Today's lesson is on snakes. Let's think about what we already know about snakes. Take out a piece of paper and draw a snake in the middle. Now, draw or write, around it, what you think you know about snakes."). Even though students in the intermediate stage may demonstrate mastery of print comprehension, oral-language and literacy development should continue to be addressed. Research indicates that allowing students to express themselves in multiple modalities, using a variety of oral and print materials and strategies, furthers comprehension and the continued development of language (National Institute for Literacy, 2007; Hoover, Klingner, Baca, & Patton, 2008).

Relevance for Diverse Learners. Students at the intermediate stage of literacy development may or may not be at an intermediate stage of language proficiency in their second (or third) language. Keeping this fact in mind, teachers should be careful to provide students with an array of literacy experiences—some of them in the student's native language. If materials (or native-language conversation opportunities) are not available within the school itself, teachers should, at a minimum, encourage students to continue speaking with parents in their native language, to identify and bring in printed materials in their native language, to interview others in the community who speak the student's native language, or to share information with their teachers and classmates about features of their native language. It is also valuable to obtain materials from local libraries, community organizations, or the Internet that provide students with a variety of literacy experiences in their native language: books, brochures, and websites in the native language as well as songs, films, and television shows. Students reading a new text in their second language (L2) can complete preview activities on related texts or topics in their native language. In using classroom practices such as these, teachers can support students' ongoing cognitive growth, ensure that their literacy development will continue on a developmentally appropriate and age-appropriate level, and provide a platform for those native-language literacy skills to transfer to English (once the student has acquired sufficient English proficiency to read, write, listen, and speak with some degree of fluency). For students who have differing abilities, also, teachers need to be mindful of students' print-literacy skills as they relate to comprehension abilities. A student with a visual-processing disability, for example, may have comprehension on a significantly higher level than is evidenced by written work or reading-assessment scores.

Accommodations will help to eliminate the barrier posed by the disability, so the student can be successful. Such accommodations might include a reader, a scribe, or access to technology that will help with reading or writing. Similarly, a student with an auditory-processing disorder may have less difficulty processing printed text but may need additional support to respond to teachers' questions in class—or to participate in a literature circle with a small group of peers, because the student has difficulty making meaning out of what is heard. Accommodations and modifications are key in ensuring the success of this population of students; close collaboration between the classroom teacher and the appropriate specialists (special educator, speech and language personnel, hearing examiner, and ESL teacher) is one effective way to achieve this goal (Hoover, Klingner, Baca, & Patton, 2008). Careful planning of classroom activities and assessments will help you to ensure that all activities are accessible to all students, whatever their needs. Consider also providing increased opportunities for students themselves to give you feedback about their needs. Students in this phase (typically mid- to late-elementary school or middle school) are often becoming increasingly aware of their own needs but may not yet have developed the confidence and self-advocacy skills to initiate a request. You can help them by soliciting their feedback and, when feasible, providing them the opportunity for input: "Did it make it easier to see when you sat in the front? Was the seat on the left side better, or the one in the middle of the front row?" Such conversations provide an opportunity for students to consider what approaches and strategies, as well as accommodations, will work for them (Chamot, 2009; Peregoy & Boyle, 2008). Their input may reveal the learning strategies that are most helpful (strategies that you can now infuse into your curriculum).

Proficient or Advanced Literacy

Overview. In the proficient or advanced literacy stage, a student reads fluently and can typically comprehend a variety of genres, texts, and levels of vocabulary (Kuder & Hasit, 2002). Students have likely developed reading strategies (and may be able to articulate or describe the strategies they use and their reasons for selecting them). Students who are proficient readers typically do not need support with basic decoding or comprehension of age-appropriate materials. However, they may continue to benefit from discussion of characters, concepts, challenges, and issues presented in readings (both fictional and non-fictional) in order to build critical thinking as well as comprehension skills (Kuder & Hasit, 2002; Peregoy & Boyle, 2008).

Relevance for Diverse Learners. As literacy is, indeed, related to second-language acquisition, issues of second-language acquisition may still exist even for proficient readers. Keep in mind that it typically takes between five and seven years (and sometimes up to ten) for cognitive academic language proficiency to develop (Cummins, 2007). Given this reality, a student who reads at a proficient level may nonetheless require support with language, vocabulary, complex or unfamiliar sentence structures, new rhetorical patterns, and unfamiliar genres. As you survey your classroom and listen to your students read, the needs of the proficient reader may be less evident than those of the student who still struggles with decoding issues. However, these students' needs are still important and can be addressed through a variety of whole-class and differentiated strategies. Consider adding enrichment activities that reinforce language and comprehension skills in areas where they might be weak; tying readings to prior knowledge and experiences; and using multiple modalities, so readers can access the language—and the meaning—of the text through a variety of modalities and intelligences. By enrichment activities, we do not mean extra handouts or worksheets. Rather, we mean real-world activities that, ideally, not only support the student's mastery of curriculum but also help build skills that will be needed beyond school. For example, a tenth-grade science teacher may need an enrichment activity to supplement a unit on cell biology. One such activity might begin with assigning students to find and read an online interview (or to view or listen to it) with a scientist engaged in scientific research at the cellular level. The students could make a web identifying key concepts or words related to cells that were mentioned in the interview. Further enrichment activities could provide the student an opportunity to list people in the school or community who are knowledgeable about cell biology, to interview those people, to summarize the interview results via video or in writing, and to create a table listing similarities and differences between the two interviews. In such an activity, students are exposed to different forms of communication and are given the opportunity to practice interactions with adults for a specific purpose in the interview. Activities such as summarizing and listing similarities or differences provide an opportunity to develop cognitive and critical-thinking skills, which are needed to interpret text. In fact, this activity could provide opportunities to develop literacy in multiple, useful ways—without ever opening an extra book or completing a worksheet. This activity is useful, also, in that it can easily be differentiated. Students who are English language learners (ELLs), or who require modifications for disability-related reasons, can research and conduct interviews in another language, can create simplified lists or word webs, can work with materials in their native language (if there are some available on the Internet), and can work with a partner. Similarly, students with disabilities can benefit from modifications and functional ways of interacting with others (for example, conducting an interview).

By valuing students' friendships and encouraging a variety of means of communication among students, teachers can provide valuable opportunities to develop language—and literacy—skills.

NEW STEPS TO TAKE—TOMORROW

1. Reflect upon your own style of reading, and comprehending, material in an unfamiliar language.

The following activity requires a little collaboration with a multilingual colleague, friend, family member, or even student. The purpose of the activity is to provide you an opportunity to reflect on the way in which you process text (visual and auditory) in an unfamiliar language—so almost any text or language will do as long as it meets that basic criterion.

First, identify a person (in one of the preceding groups) who is able to read with a fair degree of fluency in another language. Ask this individual to select a language that is unfamiliar, or slightly familiar, to you. For example, if you studied Spanish for five years in high school and college, you may have enough Spanish proficiency that the activity will not seem meaningful; you will be able to reflect best on your processing and reading style if you are working in a language that is relatively unfamiliar. If you studied French or Tagalog for six months, a year, or perhaps two years, you might be able to ask your partner to present information to you in one of those languages.

Second, ask your partner to identify a selection of text in the chosen language and to provide you with a copy of the selected text. You could use text from the Internet, a piece of literature in another language, or even functional text—instructions from your state's motor vehicle agency that have been translated into Spanish, if your state provides translations (not all do).

Third, ask your partner to read aloud to you, at a conversational pace or one that is slightly slower, from the selected text. Your purpose for listening should be to identify the main idea of the text (whether it is expository prose, fictional prose, or even poetry—though poetry may be even more confusing).

Fourth, read along with your partner and think about what elements of the text you are using to make meaning. Are you relying on syntactic clues? Listening for phonological similarities?

Finally, completing the questions in Figure 7.2 afterward should provide you with a more explicit understanding of your own processing style—which may in turn lead to increased understanding of how the process feels for your ELL students.

How to Use This Information

This activity (Figure 7.2) may give you some idea of what it feels like—cognitively and affectively—to be a second-language learner. In addition, it may also provide you with some insight into the way that you yourself process language and, therefore, may be likely to present it to others. If you process by listening to sounds, it is reasonable to anticipate you may, even subconsciously, prioritize instructional methods and strategies that focus on phonological processing and sound similarities. It is helpful to be aware of that tendency, so you can make the effort to teach in other modalities or styles if your students process differently.

Figure 7.2 How Do I Read Materials in a Second Language (L2)?

Part I. With your partner, review the following directions in preparation for reading the second-language text. Listen to your partner read the reading, and follow along as best you can with the printed text. After reading, take a moment to think about what you remember from listening and reading along. Then, respond to each of the following questions by circling the number on the Likert scale that best represents your response to the question.

When reading this text . . .

1. I sound out each unfamiliar word.

0	1	2	3
Not at all	Slightly or rarely	Somewhat	Always or almost always

2. I skip over words I do not understand.

0	1	2	3
Not at all	Slightly or rarely	Somewhat	Always or almost always

3. If I see an unfamiliar word, I reread the word.

0	1	2	3
Not at all	Slightly or rarely	Somewhat	Always or almost always

4. If I see an unfamiliar word, I think about the context before rereading the word.

0	1	2	3
Not at all	Slightly or rarely	Somewhat	Always or almost always

5. I am most comfortable if I can say words aloud.

0	1	2	3
Not at all	Slightly or rarely	Somewhat	Always or almost always

6. I find that hearing the text read aloud helps me to understand the meaning.

0	1	2	3
Not at all	Slightly or rarely	Somewhat	Always or almost always

7. I think about cognates or modern English "matches" when I read.

0	1	2	3
Not at all	Slightly or rarely	Somewhat	Always or almost always

8. I find it helpful to think about the structure of the sentence (e.g., grammar and syntax) when I am trying to find the meaning.

0	1	2	3
Not at all	Slightly or rarely	Somewhat	Always or almost always

9. I find it helpful to think about the structure of the text (e.g., poetic structure and essay structure).

0	1	2	3
Not at all	Slightly or rarely	Somewhat	Always or almost always

10. I visualize the characters or events.

0	1	2	3
Not at all	Slightly or rarely	Somewhat	Always or almost always

11. I try to reword or paraphrase each line to be sure I understand before moving on to the next one.

0	1	2	3
Not at all	Slightly or rarely	Somewhat	Always or almost always

12. I wish I could talk to someone else about the text as I read.

0	1	2	3
Not at all	Slightly or rarely	Somewhat	Always or almost always

13. I write the English words on the paper where I can.

0	1	2	3
Not at all	Slightly or rarely	Somewhat	Always or almost always

14. I can understand the meaning of the text immediately (as opposed to needing some time to think about it).

0	1	2	3
Not at all	Slightly or rarely	Somewhat	Always or almost always

Part II. Next, please rank these items from 1 to 6 in terms of which was most challenging to your personal ability to understand the reading. (*1* = least challenging; *6* = most challenging.)

Item	My Rank	Colleague's Rank
Different sounds of words		
Unfamiliar spelling		
Unfamiliar vocabulary words		
Unfamiliar grammar and syntax		
Lack of background knowledge (what the reading was about)		

Take a moment to review your responses. Can you formulate a description of what strengths and weaknesses you might bring to the process of second-language reading and processing?

Like many activities in this book, this one may be doubly profitable if you complete it and then discuss it with a colleague—either someone who has also completed it or someone who has experience with second-language reading and writing. You and that person can also collaborate to observe briefly in one another's classroom, if you'd like to, in order to gain some observational data about the literacy demands of your classroom and the way that you make language accessible to culturally and linguistically diverse exceptional (CLD/E) students. Such an observation would lead nicely into the next suggested activity for this chapter (see Figure 7.3).

2. Consider what literacy means in *your* classroom—and what the implications are for students.

Once you consider your own cognitive and linguistic context for teaching and learning, consider how that context applies to students. In this activity, we suggest that you reflectively examine one or more lessons and isolate the reading, writing, listening, and speaking demands of each, so you can determine whether your students need additional support to meet any of those demands.

How to Use This Information

The purpose of this chart (Figure 7.3) is to break down the linguistic and literacy demands of your classroom. To do this, one must first identify the expectations of the lesson in terms of writing, reading, listening, and speaking. The first column in the chart that you fill in is the area where you will note those aspects of the lesson, stated behaviorally so that you can clearly see what you are asking students to do. Once you identify the language-based components of each lesson, you are ready to move into identifying specific demands that the lesson places upon students in terms of language, literacy, and proficiency. These demands can be grouped into several categories. First, the level of proficiency required to participate in the lesson and to meet the objectives is one aspect to consider. Can a newly arrived ELL student, in the first or second stages of second-language acquisition, participate in the lesson in a meaningful way? If a student is in the intermediate proficiency stage, is necessary support provided to help that student with technical vocabulary or complex sentence structures?

Another aspect to consider is the degree to which the student must adhere to English conventions (reading, writing, spelling, listening, speaking). These conventions are often culturally bound (as in the case of turn-taking, eye contact, or collaborating with peers on written assignments) or linguistically bound (as in the case of assignments where students are graded on spelling or grammar). Again, consider these aspects of the lesson in order to make sure they are accessible to the students you currently have. If additional steps are needed, note those in the last column (under Targeted Support Needed to Help Students Meet Expectations).

As you might guess, the most important column in this chart may be the right-hand one (Targeted Support Needed to Help Students Meet Expectations), which asks you to identify specific, targeted support that will help your diverse

Figure 7.3   Examining the Literacy Demands of Your Classroom

Take a few moments to think carefully about the *current lesson or unit* you are doing with your students. What is the topic?

What is the objective (or what are the objectives)?

What is the summative assessment for the lesson?

What are the formative assessments that you will use during the lesson?

Now, having considered the objective of the lesson and the activity or skill your students will need to master by the end of it, take a few moments to note the *language and literacy demands* that this lesson places on your students.

	Expectations Placed on Students (Behavioral Statements of Tasks)	Degree of Proficiency and Fluency Required (Language Fluency and Reading Fluency)	Adherence to Convention Expected (Reading Conventions, Writing Conventions, Speaking Conventions, etc.)	Targeted Support Needed to Help Students Meet Expectations
Reading				
Writing				
Listening				
Speaking				

(Continued)

Figure 7.3 (Continued)

Following is an example section from the chart, filled out as a model to provide some guidance in filling your version out.

	Expectations Placed on Students (Behavioral Statements of Tasks)	Degree of Proficiency and Fluency Required (Language Fluency and Reading Fluency)	Adherence to Convention Expected (Reading Conventions, Writing Conventions, Speaking Conventions, etc.)	Targeted Support Needed to Help Students Meet Expectations
Reading	Students will read three pages of text. Students will identify the main idea of the text and select relevant vocabulary words for inclusion in vocabulary journals.	Students need to be able to comprehend the main idea. Students need to be able to identify vocabulary words that will be difficult for them *or* that are important for the lesson.	Students' journal does not need to adhere to grammatical convention. But the text is written in academic English at the ninth-grade level, which will be difficult for some students.	Small-group work for targeted students (during independent work time), so they can work on finding the main idea together. Teacher will follow up with each student tomorrow and review their work to make sure the correct main idea is identified. Students will receive a list of teacher-selected vocabulary words to check their choices. Definitions will be reviewed for all vocabulary words.

learners to access the lesson. This could entail providing support to a student with a disability that impacts the capacity to be successful in the lesson; it could entail making modifications to ensure the lesson is differentiated for CLD learners; it could entail a combination of those activities. You may wish to cross-check the last column you fill in against the first column you filled in (Expectations Placed on Students)—making sure the targeted support you provide is directly related to the demands of the lesson.

Once your chart is complete, cross-check the interventions or supports that you identify, thinking about them in the context of what your colleagues in ESOL (English for speakers of other languages), special education, or reading support are able to offer. You may find areas where you are able to ask a colleague for assistance that they can provide—or conversely, you may find one of your interventions or modifications to be of benefit for one of your colleagues' students as well. Another suggested use for this chart would be to make it a habit to fill it out, each day, for at least two weeks. You may not be able to do this for all of your classes, but if you are able to do it for 10 class days (two weeks), you may notice some overriding patterns in your instruction. This may enable you to see what is (or is not) facilitating learning, both for the class as a whole and for individual students. For example, you may find that you have assigned three different writing tasks in two weeks, without providing students adequate instruction about each different genre or incorporating any guided practice activities that might support them. Or you might realize that you tend to assign long sections of reading followed immediately by comprehension questions, but several of your students need supplementary activities before they are able to answer comprehension questions on their own. Sometimes seeing your plans written out, and the requirements of each lesson, can help you to identify patterns such as these and to reflect upon any adjustments you find you need to make.

3. Design activities to support a variety of literacy and language experiences.

The following activities are provided as examples of literacy-based activities that can be infused into nearly any subject area or grade-level classroom and that may be especially helpful for CLD/E students.

a. **Pen Pals.** The stereotypical conception of pen pals brings a picture to mind of students writing letters and sending them, in the mail, to some far-off country where, if all went as it should, they would receive a letter back two months later. Technology has given us the ability to communicate much more quickly. In addition, the idea of pen pals has also evolved from that era. Students can just as easily communicate with peers in another classroom down the hall, or in their own classroom. Instead of writing letters, students can keep a content-area journal (related to the subject) and can write feedback to each other. This activity can easily be adapted for very young (even preK or kindergarten students can exchange drawings) or more mature students, up to Grade 12 and even beyond.

b. **Interviews.** As described earlier in the chapter, assigning interviews is an excellent way to scaffold written-language development through first providing opportunities for oral-language use and processing. Students can interview experts in the field or, again, can interview a peer in the class about how comfortable they felt with the material and what might be most helpful. Students can design interview questions as a class, implement the interview, and have time to think about what they would like to share (or in what format they would like to share it). For example, in a history class dealing with World War II, an elementary, middle, or high school teacher can ask students to interview one another about one of several topics: what the interviewee knows about WWII (anticipation guide) or whether the interviewee has any family members who have experienced the war or who are currently soldiers (personal experience). Such assignments reinforce content and, also, help to create a feeling of community in the classroom.

c. **Center-Based Instruction.** The use of literacy centers, or stations, is increasing in popularity. Centers are a fixture in almost every elementary school classroom; however, they are still underutilized at the middle and high school levels. For teachers specifically at those levels, we recommend incorporating center-based instruction whenever possible. This may provide CLD/E students with the opportunity to access differentiated instruction and also provides support in small-group environments while students practice conventions of the English language. You could set up a reading corner in the back of the classroom, with comfortable cushions, as did one teacher of our acquaintance who set up a "story time" center in the back of his eighth-grade math classroom, where students could go to read books, current magazine articles, and young adult literature that related to mathematics. The use of the story time center became a behavioral incentive in his class, and students would frequently request that as a reward option when they finished their work or demonstrated appropriate behavior.

How to Use This Information

You may already be using these strategies. If you are, consider the way in which you deploy each strategy to ensure it is indeed equitable, relevant to CLD students, and accessible to all students regardless of ability or etiological factors. If you have not yet used any of these strategies, you may have reservations because of the need to cover material from your curriculum—which at first glance may seem unrelated to the idea of exchanging letters or reading stories. We urge you to take a holistic view of both literacy and curriculum. Indeed, research demonstrates that the integration of literacy and language-based activities into a curriculum not only supports development of reading and writing skills but also supports mastery of curriculum, providing an opportunity to make concepts and materials accessible to those students who might learn better through an online discussion than through a curriculum guide worksheet. As with many suggestions in this book, we hope that you do not feel pressure to implement each suggestion simultaneously or across the board. Rather, select one recommendation or suggestion, pilot it with a small group of students or one class, and see what the results are.

SUMMARY

As discussed in this chapter, literacy development is an ongoing process, in which teachers must consider the impact of cultural and linguistic diversity. The emergent literacy model provides a lens through which to view (and value) students' prior language, literacy, and life experiences, in order to support them as they use each of these assets to construct meaning from their reading, writing, listening, and speaking experiences. In order to support students' literacy development, it is crucial to have an understanding of the reading process; to be aware of the elements of the emergent literacy model and the stages in literacy acquisition; and to take inventory of students' life and learning experiences in formulating plans for literacy instruction. While doing each of these, teachers can also communicate with one another regarding students' strengths, literacy needs, classroom assignments, and experiences that can support the development of literacy skills across the curriculum.

EXTENSION AND COLLABORATION

1. Refer to the chart on literacy and language demands in the classroom (see Figure 7.3 Examining the Literacy Demands of Your Classroom) provided earlier in this chapter. Ask a colleague who is familiar with your curricula to check your entries after you have completed it, to ensure that you have not missed any items that should be included. Together, identify three ways that the two of you can collaborate to support diverse learners' literacy development.

2. One of the most significant ways that teachers support student understanding of text is through the use of appropriate graphic organizers. If your school has not already begun to do so, work with a colleague to coordinate the graphic organizers used in each of your classes to ensure greater consistency across grade and subject levels. One school we worked with used this idea to great advantage, introducing a common set of graphic organizers that ninth-grade core subject teachers (reading and English language arts, math, social studies, and science) could use consistently in all their classes. As the year went on, teachers noticed that the use of common materials and graphic organizers helped students to improve comprehension in all classes. Particularly for this student population, which was a highly diverse set of ninth graders, the consistency of common materials and procedures helped them to make a successful transition to the literacy demands that their different high school classes presented.

3. If one does not already exist at your school, partner with your school-based colleagues to create a literacy event for families. Parents or family members might be invited to create a book with their child or to attend a classroom or afterschool story time where families can read to their own children or others.

At-home activities might also be useful (particularly as families' ability to come to school, during or after school hours, may be limited). Students can be invited to interview family members, to create a drawing or book at home with families, or to bring in an item that "tells their family's story" and share it with the class. The purpose of any such activity is to support literacy development at home and to facilitate conversations between families and students that will help to build literacy and language skills. With these goals in mind, any activity should be structured to allow for maximum accessibility of families—an objective that will not be served by designing an activity during school hours if most of your families are unable to attend.

NEXT STEPS

Having learned about the development of literacy skills—a concept that includes comprehension of print and oral communication, including listening and speaking—you may want to consider the climate and context of your school. Supporting literacy skills in your classroom is only a piece of the puzzle. A schoolwide approach, where students have integrated language, reading, and communication experiences across all academic areas and where all staff members are perceived to value students' experiences and skills, will help to support the growth and development—and the achievement—of all learners. Some of the following suggestions may be helpful to you in thinking about how to share the information you've learned in this chapter.

COMMUNITY CONNECTIONS

1. Supporting students' literacy development often begins with providing support to families to develop and use literacy skills at home. Explore the resources your community has to offer for adult learning, adult literacy classes, and GED classes. Make sure that information about these opportunities is available—perhaps as part of a parent information center, displayed prominently both within the school and on the school website.

2. In response to many changes in information technology, libraries are becoming dynamic centers for sharing knowledge in many forms—not just repositories of books (Ferguson, 2007). Consider inviting your school's media specialist to copresent at a home and school association meeting, perhaps in conjunction with a staff member from the local community library. They could share ideas about how families can use library and media center resources (both in school and outside of school) to ensure the likelihood of collaborative and shared planning of literacy opportunities among families, teachers, and community- and school-based media specialists.

3. Often, we forget that literacy practices are not only culturally but politically bound, reflecting the beliefs and academic priorities of those in power (Freire & Macedo, 1987). Such a view may be at odds with much of what teachers are required to include in literacy instruction, where the focus is not on

political empowerment but rather on acquisition of skills according to local, state, or national standards. Still, there is room to consider students' cultural and even political contexts within school instruction. Many schools have a "word of the day" curriculum. Consider adapting this curriculum to include words that are important to students from a cultural perspective. Take time, in your lessons, to discuss current events and highlight those words or concepts that are important to your students' daily lives (such as might be found in an article on poverty, for example, or violence in a community). Freire states also that, to be most effective, literacy instruction should be based on realities, concepts, and words that are most important in students' daily lives and that encourage them to recognize their own potential (Freire, 1993). Even if you cannot determine the subject matter or vocabulary words that you are required to teach, you can support your students in developing their awareness of their own context within the larger community. When you preteach vocabulary for your next unit, give students a list with definitions and ask them to find connections between each word and their own lives. Suggest that they go home and interview their parents, asking their parents to put the words in order from most important to least important—or if the words are technical vocabulary, from most familiar to least familiar. Encourage students to consider which words they are likely to use outside school and which ones represent school-only vocabulary (*working class* as opposed to *agrarian*, for example). Each of these activities not only supports students' literacy development but also helps them to make connections between their own reality and that of the larger community that they inhabit.

USEFUL WEBSITES

- Center for Applied Linguistics' Literacy Page: www.cal.org/topics/le. The Center for Applied Linguistics maintains a page of literacy resources applicable specifically to second-language learners.
- International Reading Association: www.ira.org. The International Reading Association has a variety of resources about reading and literacy, including materials for families as well as free lesson plans produced through a partnership with the National Council of Teachers of English.
- National Council of Teachers of English: www.readwritethink.org/ student_mat/index.asp. While the site might seem to be focused exclusively on language arts teachers, it contains a variety of useful information on literacy development and instructional practices.
- National Center for Learning Disabilities: www.ncld.org. The NCLD conducts research and advocacy for children and adults with learning differences. Their website contains a number of resources related to policy, advocacy, and reading, particularly relevant for students whose literacy development may be impacted by a learning difference.
- National Reading Panel: www.nationalreadingpanel.org. This website contains a wealth of research related to literacy development, as well as a summary and downloadable copy of *Teaching Children to Read*, the most recent report of the panel on literacy practices.

8 Assessment

How Do You Know What Your Students Know?

Robert, a fifteen-year veteran, had recently been asked by his principal to mentor a new teacher in the building. Sylvia had just graduated from her teacher preparation program and was preparing to set up her classroom. Before the first day of school, Robert stopped by to help her. He found Sylvia staring at the district's lesson plan form.

"Do I have to fill this out every day?" she asked.

"Yes," Robert responded. "Really, the most important categories are the objective, the instructional sequence, and your assessment."

"So in the assessment box, I can just write my test or quiz or whatever I'm doing that day?"

"No," said Robert. "You should include formative assessment that will tell you how students are learning at each phase of the lesson. Things like, are you observing as your students work? Are you listening while they talk in small groups? Are you reading over their shoulders as they write their answers down?"

Sylvia put down her plan book and looked up at him. "Well, maybe you can answer this, then. Ever since I took assessment in college, I've had this question. To me, all of that is just good teaching. When you get right down to it, what's the difference between assessment and just plain good teaching?"

THE ISSUES

- Purpose and types of assessment
- Validity and reliability of assessment for culturally and linguistically diverse (CLD) students
- Impact of second-language acquisition issues on assessment
- Formal and informal assessment measures appropriate for English language learners (ELLs)
- Standardized-assessment bias and alternative measures for classroom use

122

QUESTIONS TO CONSIDER

1. What is the answer to Sylvia's question? In other words, how does assessment relate to instruction?

2. How can Sylvia know whether her tests and quizzes are really measuring what they are supposed to measure?

3. How does formative assessment differ from summative assessment in the information it provides about student understanding?

4. What considerations should Sylvia take into account when she plans both formative and summative assessment? What issues relating to culturally and linguistically diverse exceptional (CLD/E) students should be considered?

GETTING THE ANSWERS

Understanding Assessment

Assessment, these days, is a term most commonly associated with high-stakes testing. The reality, however, is that assessment in the classroom should be as natural, and as common, as breathing. Assessment is the logical outgrowth of instruction, and in fact, assessment within the educational setting refers to the process a teacher uses to determine the scope, content, pacing, and effectiveness of instruction. An accurate understanding of assessment is essential to designing and implementing this tool appropriately in the classroom—and as Sylvia pointed out in the vignette above, good assessment is closely tied to instruction. For example, the purpose of assessing a student for special education eligibility is different from that which a teacher might have when trying to determine a student's comfort level and familiarity with printed material when the child has just entered the school system. Because the two assessments would have a different purpose—as the teacher needs different information and will use the information in different ways in each situation—the form and processes associated with each assessment will likely be different as well. In general, assessment has many purposes, and the teacher must be aware of the purpose for it to be effective (Taylor, 2009)

To further delineate the issues at play in an example such as this, the following paragraphs provide an overview of the purposes, forms, interpretation, and core principles of assessment.

Purposes of Assessment

No assessment is done without determining what purpose exists for the assessment. ("What did I want to know?" "What did I intend to measure?" or "What did I find out or purport to find out?") Another way to put this is, "Why am I trying to find out information? What will I use this information for?" Not doing so is like asking, "What do I want to wear today?" and picking something out of one's closet without first considering what one will be doing, what the weather is like, and other factors that will undoubtedly impact your answer to that question.

Without an answer to this question, there is no need to proceed; each assessment should have a purpose that is clear to the teacher prior to the beginning of the process. The purpose of assessment might be to plan for future instruction; to evaluate learning up to a particular point; to screen for special education eligibility or ESOL services; or to monitor progress in order to determine appropriate interventions. If you are conducting an assessment and have not yet identified the purpose, we suggest stopping and revisiting your objective in order to identify your purpose in assessing students at that point. Suggestions for doing so are provided in the following paragraphs.

Identifying the purpose of assessment involves asking what you (or the professionals involved) plan to do with the information you gain. If you intend to use it to decide what to teach the next day based on what your students have learned already, that is your purpose. If you intend to use the information to evaluate a child's year-end learning in order to make a decision about placement for the following year, then your purpose is different. Chances are, the information you collect, and the procedures you use to collect it, will be different as well.

Consider the examples in Figure 8.1, and jot your thoughts down in the margins. If you have a colleague reading the chapter at the same time as you, review your answers with your coworker in addition to checking your work at the end of the chart.

Note that assessment is often conducted, and information used, for multiple purposes, particularly for classroom teachers who use multiple sources of information to make decisions (Reynolds, Livingston, & Willson, 2009). Accordingly, in Figure 8.1, Number 3 could also be answered as "measurement of learning over time," and Number 4 could be answered as "gathering information to plan instruction for the next day," though a cumulative test is more likely to supply information about unit-level planning than day-to-day instruction. As with many things in teaching, though, the answer can often be seen as a combination of factors. Figure 8.2 on page 133 references some of the different concepts that relate to the assessment process and describes their relevance for diverse learners.

Forms of Assessment

In addition to having a variety of purposes, assessment can also take different forms. *Formal* and *informal* are terms used to describe the form that an assessment takes.

Types of Formal Assessment

A *formal assessment* is the use of a standardized process or instrument to gain information, typically at a single point in time, about a student's status or progress with respect to academics, social or emotional well-being, cognitive ability, or other factors (definition adapted from Council of Chief State School Officers [CCSSO], 2009). The CCSSO notes that formal assessment is

Figure 8.1	Purposes of Assessment

Directions: Match the most likely purpose to each assessment scenario:

_____ 1. Roberto is a new student at Kenwood Elementary. The school refers him to the county's ESOL office, where he is given a battery of written- and oral-language proficiency tests.

_____ 2. At the end of her math class, Stacie asks her students to jot their questions on index cards and hand them in as they leave the room.

_____ 3. Ling is placed on a behavior-management plan. At the end of the day, she and her teacher sit down together and review her behavior for the day. They fill out a checklist describing her behavior and then read her behavioral goals together to determine if she has met them for the day.

_____ 4. Umberto, a fifth-grade resource teacher, plans a life-skills unit for his students and tells them they will have a cumulative test on the unit at the end of the week.

_____ 5. Because of concerns about Katerina's performance in math, her teacher requests testing from the school's prereferral intervention team. As Katerina was placed in the prereferral process earlier in the year without measurable gains, the team decides to move forward with academic achievement and cognitive testing.

    A. Progress monitoring

    B. Special education eligibility determination

    C. Determination of language proficiency

    D. Gathering information to plan instruction for the next day

    E. Measurement of learning over time

Answers: 1: C. 2: D. 3: A. 4: E. 5: B.

often, but not always, implemented as a standardized written assessment; though, particularly for young children, oral assessment or even observation protocols can also be used. Some states and districts are moving toward the use of portfolio assessment, using a standardized rubric, to capture a greater range of knowledge and competency on the part of the student (CCSSO, 2009). From the perspective of educators who work with CLD students, there are serious concerns about the validity or reliability of formal, standardized assessments with English language learner (ELL) students (Pennock-Roman & Rivera, 2007; Baca & Cervantes, 2004). Variables of culture, language, prior schooling, exposure to literacy, and socioeconomic status can all impact the way in which a student performs on such assessments and should be taken into consideration when in the assessment process, particularly if the student is from a population different from that on which the test was normed (Hoover, Klingner, Baca, & Patton, 2008). Particularly under current education policy—which requires newly arrived ELLs to begin taking state math examinations to determine AYP (adequate yearly progress) within the first year of arrival and reading examinations after only a year in the United States—students' test scores may be more indicative of their grasp of English language, their experience with the American school system, and their test-taking skills, than of any actual content knowledge. Such assessments can indeed provide valuable information regarding language, school experience, and test-taking skills, among other factors. However, teachers must use extreme caution when considering these tests as indicators of cognitive ability, academic skills or motivation, or appropriate educational placement.

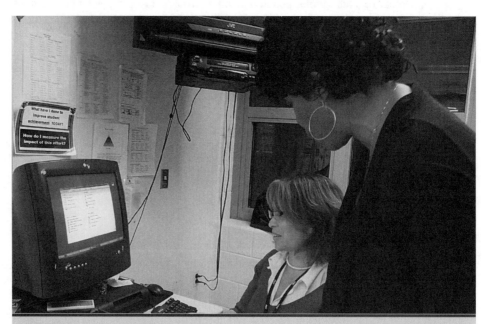

Looking together at students' performance data can help teachers in different roles identify strategies to support learning across content areas.

An *informal assessment* is a process or instrument used to gain information about a child's status or progress without standardized testing or formal assessment (Taylor, 2009). Informal assessment may involve consideration of factors including observation, conversation with a student, student completion of teacher-made worksheets, activities, and tests, a piece of student writing, completion of homework, a prelesson survey or anticipation guide, and numerous other classroom activities. Stiggins and Conklin (1992) make the compelling point that, while high-stakes testing occupies much of the public interest, it accounts for something along the lines of 1% of instructional time, while informal assessments (measured in terms of instructional time) account for 99% of the assessments teachers conduct.

Types of Informal Assessment

You may see the following informal assessments used in your school. Each can provide information that may supplement or even contradict that which is gained from standardized assessment, particularly for CLD/E learners.

Observation. Consider what you have learned about behavioral observation in Chapter 4 of this text. When practiced correctly, behavioral observation can provide you a great deal of information regarding student understanding and mastery of skills. Observing your students as they listen to you and to classmates, as they complete assignments, and as they work in small groups with peers will help you assess the degree to which they are able to meet objectives.

Class Work. You can assess students' knowledge and skills based on work completed in class, as well: notes taken, worksheets finished, group activities completed. Keep in mind, though, the limitations of informal assessment based on class work. As these activities are completed in the classroom, environmental factors such as noise and temperature, as well as time constraints, may make it difficult to concentrate and may impact a student's performance. Relationships with peers may affect (positively or negatively) a student's ability to complete a group task. Students who need additional processing time (whether for language-learning reasons or because of disability) may perform at lower levels on work that must be completed during the class session, as they may not have processing time and may also be limited by anxiety due to that fact. In our experience, some students may reach a point of frustration; assuming that they will never finish, so it is not worthwhile for them to try. Such results should be considered with caution, therefore, as the assessment may be more indicative of the student's prior experience with assessment, affective response, anxiety, processing speed, linguistic processing, or numerous other factors, as opposed to indicating the student's mastery of content with any degree of accuracy.

Reviewing portfolios with students, or with parents, provides a valuable way to initiate conversations about students' progress, strengths, and areas for development.

Classroom Tests and Quizzes. You can assess a student's knowledge based on teacher-made assessments, including tests and quizzes. Many of the same limitations of class work will also apply to tests and quizzes. Teachers should be aware of potential complications such as test anxiety. And any test or quiz should be reviewed, before you give it, for linguistic and cognitive accessibility to ensure it is appropriate to the needs of your population. An example may help to illustrate why this is important. In a third-grade class that one of us observed some years ago, a teacher gave students a quiz that instructed them to compare rainfall amounts in two cities. The directions instructed students to "refer to the table to find the answer." Upon reaching this point in the assessment, one student began moving the chair back and forth, stretching to see the other side of the table, and looking under the table and on each of the table legs. The teacher approached the student and asked, "Why are you fidgeting?" The student replied, "The test says to look on the table to find the answer!" As in this example, keep in mind that your test directions, as well as the content language, must be accessible to all students, particularly those who are linguistically or culturally diverse, who process information differently, or who have diverse abilities.

Essays or Other Writing Assignments. Frequently, educators use written assignments (essays, poems, reflection journals, and the like) to assess student knowledge. Such a choice has the advantage of allowing students to select the manner in which they present the information they know, and (depending on the assignment) it may provide the opportunity for students to focus on aspects of the subject that they understand best and feel most comfortable with. By the same token, one must also consider what is being assessed. Frequently, for ELLs and students with special education needs, essay assignments (particularly lengthy ones) may turn out to be an assessment of language proficiency, writing fluency, and organizational skills as much as (or more than) content. Consider providing scaffolds for these students if you administer such an assessment: graphic organizers, outlines, skeletal paragraphs (paragraphs with some text already written in; the amount of text provided can be decreased over time as the student's writing skills develop). Providing outlines and graphic organizers may also allow you to assess a student's content knowledge based on those documents, even if the individual is not able to complete the full writing task. Finally, consider the sensory and graphomotor demands of writing. For students who find it difficult to write legibly, or to write within a small space, we strongly recommend allowing them to type written assignments, dictate into an audio recorder, use computer-transcription programs, or use a scribe accommodation.

Discussion or Oral Questioning. For students with limited writing proficiency, or who take extra time to complete written assignments, it may be helpful to assess comprehension orally through question-and-answer sessions, through listening as the student explains a process, or through observing a small- or large-group discussion. Bear in mind that, just as written assignments become tests of writing skills, an assessment based on oral performance is as much an assessment of oral-language skills, interpersonal dynamics, and pragmatic understanding as it is of content. Particularly when working with ELLs or students with disabilities—each of whom, for different reasons, may be unfamiliar with "typical" behaviors during teacher-student conversation in the United States—provide a welcoming environment, be aware of the student's comfort level and anxiety, and provide the student adequate response time. Again, keep in mind the central principle of knowing your students' strengths and backgrounds and being aware of what your assessment purports to measure in order to make sure that you are really measuring it.

Small-Group Tasks. Frequently, assessing a student's small-group performance involves a mix of other informal assessment procedures. Small-group activities are often a blend of written and oral tasks, asking students to discuss a problem with peers and produce a written solution. In addition to all of the issues outlined above, pay attention to the interpersonal dynamics of your small groups. Does each student feel comfortable working with the students in the group? Are there cultural differences that may impact communication styles? Do students of one particular gender or culture always seem to be placed in leadership roles? If so, what reasons might account for that fact, and what might you do to ensure equity in group roles while also helping students to feel secure with their ability to contribute? Are directions understandable to each member of the group? Are roles clearly assigned, or are students left to figure out what they should be doing at any given time?

The answers to any of these questions, on their own, could impact the success of a group or of a single student within it.

Portfolio Assessment. Portfolio assessment is becoming increasingly popular at the classroom level as well (Taylor, 2009). Portfolio assessment provides teachers an avenue to examine students' work based on a number of work samples, collected over an extended period of time, in order to gain a sense of the student's growth or attainment of mastery. We strongly advocate the use of portfolio assessment—particularly portfolios that incorporate multiple modalities, such as constructed writing, oral expression, song, dance, and art. Standardized-assessment results may be included as part of a portfolio but are not required. The contents of a portfolio are largely determined by the purpose of the portfolio. Educators typically group portfolios into three types: developmental (showing learning or demonstrating a process over time), assessment (demonstrating a student's competency in relation to particular benchmarks or objectives), and showcase (displaying the best of a student's work, determined according to specific criteria outlined by the teacher *or* the student). There are further resources on portfolios in Useful Websites at the end of this chapter. As with any form of assessment, the validity of portfolio assessment can be limited by the nature of the items included—particularly if the selection criteria are influenced by linguistically, culturally, or cognitively biased requirements such as grammatical proficiency, mechanics, neatness, or even completeness. Assignments themselves can be biased as well, placing students in a situation where, for reasons beyond their control, students are not able to demonstrate competence due to the linguistic bias of an assignment. (For example, consider

Teachers can review student work in order to assess comprehension and plan for the next lesson.

the math quiz discussed earlier in this chapter, which asked the student to refer to the table. Had that quiz been included in the student's portfolio, it would not have provided an accurate depiction of the student's mathematical understanding at that point in time.) It is for this reason that we strongly recommend including a variety of materials, collected in a variety of settings over time, in a portfolio. Together, the contents of the portfolio can provide a balanced view of the student's competency, compensating for the potential linguistic or cultural bias of any one assignment in particular.

Skits and Storytelling. As with group work, skits, reenactments, and storytelling can help students to demonstrate content knowledge. However, reenactments and skits also allow ELLs (or students who have difficulty speaking in class, for any number of reasons) to participate with a minimal amount of speaking. These students can play nonspeaking roles—or you can ask the class to construct a pantomime of a scientific process or political event. Such assessments have the advantage of allowing students to build linguistic and social skills while demonstrating knowledge of content and participating successfully with a group of their peers. In this way, such assessments also help to support students' self-perception and encourage them to take academic risks in a safe, peer-supported environment.

Drawing. For students who may lack expressive language proficiency, drawing can be a highly effective way of demonstrating what they know. Students can draw a scene from a story, a historical event, a scientific process, or their own reaction to anything discussed in class. Drawings can be highly complex and prepared over time—or can be sketched quickly on a blank page of notebook paper if that fits your classroom needs better. (A two-minute "sketch break" in the midst of a teacher lecture or minilesson can help students refocus while also providing them the opportunity to demonstrate what they know—and providing *you* the opportunity to see what they know through the use of formative assessment.) As with all activities, students' success may be largely dependent on your ability to provide clear directions. Make sure students know exactly what you are looking for—provide directions orally and in writing, and model how to follow them as well. If possible, allow students to share their drawings with one another or with the whole class—having had the opportunity to draw ideas may help a student to feel more comfortable sharing them (particularly with the drawing present as a reference). This may also help to scaffold oral-language proficiency. For students who are still emerging as writers, consider asking them to draw and then write a few words, or a sentence, about their drawing. (Drawing is an excellent learning strategy—so if you choose to use it in your classroom, take time to talk about why you are having students draw and how drawing can help them to remember ideas as a way of reinforcing metacognitive skills).

Homework. We frequently see lessons in which teachers' summative assessment or follow-up activity involves completion of a task for homework, to be reviewed the next day. This may seem logical from one standpoint: What better way to know whether a student "owns" a skill than to ask the child to perform the relevant task independently after the lesson? However, for CLD/E students, homework frequently becomes an assessment of home support rather than of content knowledge. Students whose families face financial stress, separation of family members, demands of multiple jobs in and out of the home, or uncertainty about their futures may find that, once they get home, the responsibilities associated with those demands leave them little time to be students. In our experience, it is not uncommon for students to go straight from school to work for four or five hours, then home, where they are responsible for feeding younger siblings, supervising them (helping them with their own homework) and putting them to bed, and only then having the time and availability to consider their own schoolwork. Such students, whose homework time begins at midnight or even later, if at all, should not be penalized for coming to school without doing their homework. In the same way, students with disabilities that result in a need for extra time may find it stressful to come home from eight hours of school, only to find that they must begin their homework immediately if they are to have any hope of finishing it before the next day starts. Such students may benefit far more from time to process their day, reorganize themselves cognitively and emotionally, and prepare for the following day than from completing additional math problems or comprehension questions. If you assign and grade homework on a regular basis, make sure that you are familiar with your students' family situations and make allowances for those who lack the flexibility to complete homework as the "typical" student would. We know several teachers who assign daily homework but make themselves available during lunch, so students can complete homework in their rooms if they are not able to stay after school due to family or job obligations. Keep in mind, though, that each student has only one lunch period and, even with teacher support, likely will not be able to complete four or more daily homework assignments in that one lunch period. Bear in mind, also, that lunch and recess are not extra time but are purposeful and necessary activities: Students who are forced, through no fault of their own, to work through that break time will find themselves at a disadvantage when lunch is over and class time resumes.

Interpreting Assessments of Diverse Learners

In considering the appropriateness of any assessments (formal or informal) for diverse learners, one must keep several factors in mind. Formal assessments such as the Woodcock-Johnson, the Wechsler Intelligence Scale for Children (WISC), and other standardized measures of intelligence and achievement are not normed on ELL populations (Pennock-Roman & Rivera, 2007), and therefore the results are not valid for those populations.

For ELLs, formal assessment may be most appropriately used to establish a baseline for achievement in the United States or to test English language performance, rather than to evaluate the quality or relevance of the student's prior schooling. Of course, even if used to provide baseline data, a test cannot be used to provide formal information in a way different from that which was intended by the instrument's creator. For example, a teacher can look at a student's low reading achievement score and draw an informal conclusion, supported by other observational data, that the score has been impacted by the student's developing English proficiency. However, that teacher cannot look at the reading achievement score

Figure 8.2	Key Terminology Related to Assessment

Norming: The process of collecting data over several administrations in order to ensure the test results are consistent, reliable, and valid (see below). Standardized tests are typically not normed on ELL students, so the results may not be valid for that group of students.

Reliability: The degree to which an assessment can be repeated consistently over time. For example, if an observation protocol is followed strictly each time an observer visits a student, then the observation is a reliable qualitative assessment. However, if the observer works without following specific guidelines or criteria, then the assessment loses reliability. The observer could take notes one time but not another; could focus on a child's attentiveness one time and the affective response to peers another time; or any number of different constructs (Reynolds, Livingston, & Willson, 2009).

Validity: The degree to which an assessment measures what it purports to measure. For example, a physical education test that is administered entirely on paper cannot validly measure a child's actual physical ability or athletic skill. Rather, that test measures the child's writing and reading (and perhaps test-taking) skills with respect to physical education concepts. Similarly, if a child who is new to the United States (but who has had seven years of prior schooling) scores poorly on a reading exam, it is very possible that the child can indeed read and write but cannot do so with fluency on a test administered in English (Reynolds, Livingston, & Willson, 2009).

Standardized or norm-referenced: Refers to an assessment in which a student's performance is calculated relative to all other students who took the test. Scores are often reported as a percentile, representing the number of test takers who received a score below the student's. Thus, a score in the 90th percentile on a norm-referenced test such as the PSAT does not mean the student answered 90% of questions correctly. Rather, it means the student had more correct answers than 90% of the students who took the test (Losardo & Notari-Syverson, 2001).

Criteria-referenced: Unlike a norm-referenced assessment, a criteria-referenced assessment is one in which a student's performance is evaluated based on the ability to accomplish specific tasks, which are often dictated by a school or district curriculum sequence. For example, a student whose essay was scored with a rubric for clarity, organization, and supporting detail was evaluated using a criteria-referenced assessment (Losardo & Notari-Syverson, 2001).

Idiographic: Idiographic data attempts to describe characteristics of an individual in relation to one or more standards, criteria, or tasks. Idiographic data may include, for example, observations, student work products, informal reading assessments, and running records, all of which are phrased descriptively ("She is five feet tall and has blond hair." "She completed the reading task successfully with no missed words").

Nomothetic: Nomothetic data attempts to describe characteristics of a class or group, using measures that are applicable to the entire group and can be administered to the entire group. Nomothetic data often provides a quantitative picture of a group's skills (or of the skills of an individual in relation to the group). Nomothetic data is not phrased descriptively but provides measurements that apply to a group or an individual. ("She is in the 80th percentile for height." "Her hair color is similar to that of 30% of the population." "Her reading score was in the third stanine.")

Dynamic assessment: Dynamic assessment is an interactive process, in which the nature and content of the assessment itself can change in response to the student's input or responses. Dynamic assessment is closely tied to responsive instruction and can be used as a type of formative assessment to measure student learning and to help determine the next step in instruction.

and extrapolate from it to provide an objective score or measure of the child's English language proficiency. A reading test is not designed to yield objective scores about language proficiency—only about reading proficiency—and even then, only within the parameters of culturally and linguistically appropriate administration.

Informal assessment, unlike formal assessment, provides the teacher an opportunity to gear an assessment toward a student's strengths. If a student does not have the written-language proficiency to complete a unit-end test, the teacher can still measure content knowledge by asking questions orally, asking the student to sketch out or reenact parts of the reading, or observing as the student completes a task. Informal assessments can be more appropriate than formal assessments for many diverse learners, particularly in situations where formal assessments would put students with linguistic, cultural, physiological, or learning differences at a disadvantage (Losardo & Notari-Syverson, 2001). However, care must still be used when examining the results of any one assessment in particular; looking at multiple sources is likely to give the best indication of patterns in a student's responses over time and in multiple testing situations. Later in the chapter (see Figure 8.6 on page 141), we provide a list of questions teachers should ask when considering the results of any standardized assessment administered to a culturally or linguistically diverse student (or for that matter, to any student—some of the questions are not specific solely to culture and language).

In addition to knowing key concepts about the purposes, forms, and types of assessment, there are also some core principles (implicit in some of the discussion above) that must be kept in mind for teachers conducting any assessment activities—whether formal or informal, standardized or criteria-referenced. We summarize them in the following paragraphs.

Core Principles for Assessing Diverse Learners

1. *There is no such thing as a language-free assessment.* The impact of linguistic diversity cannot be overstated in the assessment process. Students in the process of second-language acquisition can find the unfamiliar directions, unfamiliar vocabulary, and unfamiliar syntax and structure of English assessments to be challenging, confusing, and inaccessible. Students who have language-based disabilities, or other disabilities that impact the processing of language, may process the language of the test more slowly and, therefore, receive a result that does not accurately speak to their knowledge of the subject matter. Finally, affective or emotional barriers, such as anxiety or negative prior experience, may make it difficult for students to process the language of the assessment. Therefore, they may also receive scores that do not reflect their knowledge, skills, or abilities.

2. *There is no such thing as a culture-free assessment.* A picture vocabulary test that asks students to "point to the chapel," for example, is culturally biased on several counts. Some students may not know what a chapel is; for some students, the act of pointing is culturally unacceptable, and their hesitation to follow the directions might well arise from a hesitation to violate an important cultural norm as opposed to an inability to identify the chapel or to understand the directions.

3. *Assessments are often based on biased assumptions regarding developmental norms, communication styles, and family support and structure.* American school

systems, from preschool on, typically require children to be self-toileting, self-feeding, and self-dressing. Such standards for self-care and independence are not universal. Many cultures rely on a different set of developmental norms, with caregivers feeding children well into their third or fourth year and with children needing significant assistance to get dressed even several years into their primary school experience. In some cultures, children are not encouraged to speak up, to request items before they are offered, or to speak if they have not been directly spoken to. Families may be more or less involved in the educational process, depending on their cultural background and their socioeconomic needs. Developmental scales used to screen for developmental disabilities, cognitive delays, and language delays may not take such diversity into account, thereby causing potential bias in the process and placing students at risk of over- or underidentification for special education placement.

4. *Assessment requires a knowledge of the "whole child" (Baca & Cervantes, 2004), including the child's background, home culture and country, prior schooling, mental and physical wellness, and family situation.* A child who is carrying significant responsibilities at home may have difficulty completing homework or staying awake in classes, but not from a lack of knowledge, ability, or motivation.

5. *Assessment is an ongoing and dynamic process, requiring identification of a pattern of behavior cognitively, physically, socially, linguistically, perceptually, and academically.* A culturally, linguistically, and etiologically appropriate assessment must be grounded in the belief that no single test or instrument can give a complete picture of a child's functioning; that the choice of assessments, or the manner in which they are administered, may be altered (if possible) based on the responses received from the student; and that information from the assessment can be used to inform the assessment process itself, subsequent interventions, and decisions regarding instruction.

NEW STEPS TO TAKE—TOMORROW

1. Evaluate your own assessment practices.

Consider the ways in which you assess student learning in your classroom—both for the short term and for the long term. Which assessments do you choose and control as the classroom teacher (for example, classroom-based activities)? Which assessments do you have little or no control over (such as standardized tests)? Where you have control, are you using these core principles in such a way that your assessment practices are culturally and linguistically appropriate? How are you using assessment results in your instructional planning?

We recommend listing the assessments you use in a particular lesson or unit, and considering their potential limitations as well as their assets. Does the range of assessments in your lesson allow you to gain a sense of each student's mastery? Can you accurately gauge whether each student has met the objective, and if not, can you identify exactly which element or task is presenting the challenge?

We provide a model format for thinking about your assessments (see Figure 8.3). This model assumes a hypothetical third-grade math class with

Figure 8.3	Planning Guide: Assessment Methods, Limitations, and Ways to Offset Limitations (Model)

Assessment Method	Limitation	Ways to Offset Limitation
I will observe as students listen to teacher explanation of strategies.	Involves making inferences about which student is listening or how a student shows understanding.	I will check for understanding expressively ("Mokhtar, can you tell me how to do this strategy?") and receptively ("Lift up your pen if you feel ready to try using this strategy."). I will use additional methods of assessment to check for comprehension.
I will observe as students write answers on worksheets during whole-class explanation.	Other factors could account for a student not writing the answer: lack of English proficiency, not understanding directions, graphomotor or fine motor challenges, fatigue, or stress.	If I observe a student not writing, I will review directions. I will ask the child to tell me the answer orally. If a student appears to be fatigued or under stress, I will monitor this throughout the period and will pull the student aside at the end of class to make sure everything is OK. I can also ask the counselor and other teachers who work with the student if they notice anything wrong. If a student appears to have motor difficulties with writing, perhaps I can let the child use a marker on a whiteboard (which may be easier to grasp), or tell answers to a peer, who can write for the student.
I will listen as students share answers with each other to check their work.	If students are not sharing answers, it could be because they do not feel comfortable talking with that peer; because they understand the strategy but cannot explain it; or because they are not sure what to do or whether it is OK to talk in class.	I will review the directions with the whole class and with pairs if students appear not to be working. I will review my partner pairings before class so that I can identify any potential cultural issues (e.g., some students being uncomfortable with opposite-gender partners) before the class. I will encourage students to write the answer out in "math language" (i.e., numbers) for their partners if they are having difficulty explaining it in words, and then use the numbers as a basis for talking. I will also use other methods of assessment to complement this one.
I will observe as students raise their hands to answer questions in whole-class review of partner work.	Other factors could account for a student not raising a hand: culture, personality, shyness, lack of confidence about the right answer, or fatigue.	I will provide a "brain break" after a few minutes of whole-class review, where I ask students to list or draw one thing they have learned so far. I will call on an equal variety of students but will give students needed wait time and will be mindful of culture and learning issues in selecting who I ask to speak to the whole class. (For example, if I call on a student with an expressive language disorder, I will give advance notice and will structure the question in such a way that the answer can be read word for word from a notebook.) I will also use other methods of assessment, so if a student does not respond to this portion of the lesson, I have other means of knowing whether the objective was attained.

Assessment Method	Limitation	Ways to Offset Limitation
I will observe as students list or draw one thing they have learned so far.	Students need to understand directions to perform well here. Two minutes may not be enough time for students to process directions and actually draw or write.	I will post directions on the overhead as well as repeating them and will circulate to make sure each student understands. If students appear to need additional time, I will extend the brain break to four minutes.
I will observe as students complete the remainder of worksheet problems independently.	Other factors could impact performance: attention, fatigue, understanding directions, difficulties with computation (as opposed to strategy), fine motor or graphomotor issues.	I will allow students to take a restroom break if they need it before beginning this part of the assessment. If students are not able to complete this assessment, I will pull them aside to work with them one-on-one to determine what the difficulty might be. If students appear to have difficulty with computation but know the strategy, I will allow them to explain the strategy to me orally and then check the computations with a calculator.

about 20 students. Fifty percent of the students are ELLs and three of the students have IEPs or 504 plans with accommodations (one of the ELL students is dually coded). Students are learning strategies for double-digit multiplication; the objective is, "Students will identify and select a strategy for double-digit multiplication." Figure 8.3 is a chart listing the various methods of assessment that the teacher will use throughout the lesson, along with the potential limitations of each and a suggestion for offsetting, or compensating for, the limitation.

As you can see from the amount of text in Figure 8.3, this process is time consuming, especially the first time you try it. However, we highly recommend that you try writing the steps out for at least one lesson, and incorporate this thought process into your planning for every lesson. If you coteach or work with a paraprofessional, ask your partner to review the chart with you, as our colleagues can often see the areas we may miss, due to differences in approaches, perspectives, background, and learning styles.

A blank copy of the chart is provided in Figure 8.4 for your reference.

How to Use This Information

As this chart suggests (see Figure 8.3), there is no "perfect assessment." Before assessing, one must first ask, "For what child?" "At what time in the student's life?" and "For what purpose?" Every assessment has its built-in bias and limitations. In classroom teaching, the key is to acknowledge those limitations and "triangulate" your assessment, using other sources to provide you information and supplement the data you gain from that particular one.

Once you have filled in this chart for one lesson (or unit, you can use it as long-term planning for your formal unit assessments as well), consider the

| Figure 8.4 | Planning Guide: Assessment Methods, Limitations, and Ways to Offset Limitations (Blank) |

Assessment Method	Limitation	Ways to Offset Limitation

generalizability of what you have written. It is likely that, if one pair-share activity has limitations in your classroom as an assessment tool, then your other pair-share activities may have similar limitations. Use the information in this chart as a guide to identify areas where you can increase the accessibility and appropriateness of your assessments—or plan to replace or compensate for assessments that are not culturally and linguistically accessible.

As with many items in this book, this chart will be most effective if you take the time to share it with those colleagues who also share your students and your planning. Your paraprofessionals, your coteachers, and the members of your department or grade-level team (who teach the same students or the same content) may all benefit from seeing your thoughts, and they may also adopt some of your recommendations and compensatory strategies in order to make assessment more reliable across the curriculum.

2. Add informal assessments that are CLD/E friendly.

The chart in Figure 8.5 summarizes benefits that specific informal assessments or activities may have for CLD/E learners. Read through the chart, and identify those assessments that you are not using currently. Select one each week, and try it out in your classes.

Figure 8.5 Informal Assessments Beneficial to Culturally and Linguistically Diverse Exceptional (CLD/E) Students

Assessment	Benefits for CLD/E Students
Observation	Teachers are able to observe student behaviors, and language production, in several different settings or while completing several different tasks in order to provide a measure of skills.
Heterogeneous small groups	Small-group work, with students who have a higher degree of language proficiency, may help ELLs to access content more readily than in whole-class instruction. Peers can help ELL students find words to "put to" the concepts they may already know. The students' performance in this setting may, therefore, be a more reliable indicator of knowledge or skills than a whole-class or independent assessment.
Song or performance	Under Gardner's (2000) multiple intelligence theory, use of music helps to develop students' cognitive skills for future learning and also allows them to demonstrate knowledge and understanding that may not be as evident in their writing or oral language. For this reason, using music for assessment as well as instruction is a valuable strategy (Armstrong, 2000).
Visual representation or art	As with music or performance, asking students to express knowledge in multiple modalities (using diverse intelligences) can be effective for diverse learners (Armstrong, 2000). Allowing students to draw or diagram their knowledge also removes the barrier of language.
Journaling	Journals are easily differentiated for students' language proficiency, writing skill, comprehension, and prior knowledge. Journals can be evaluated on the basis of completion and on the basis of adherence to predetermined (perhaps differentiated) standards. In lieu of journals, students can record responses on sticky notes and attach them to book pages for use in discussion.

(Continued)

| Figure 8.5 | (Continued) |

Assessment	Benefits for CLD/E Students
Portfolio	Portfolio assessment can support the needs of CLD/E students by allowing them to assemble their best work over time or to document their growth toward a particular objective or set of objectives.
Exit cards	Asking students to complete an exit ticket (a card or paper handed in at the end of a lesson listing a question, a fact learned in the lesson, or an exciting connection the student noticed) provides a useful summary of what students have learned and what still needs to be taught. ELLs may benefit because the card is confidential, providing a way to ask questions, and does not require extensive linguistic production (a student can complete an exit card by writing a word or even drawing a picture).
Student self-assessment	Students can track their own understanding and their own perceived mastery, using response journals, cards, a chart, stickers, or other means. This not only allows teachers to see students' level of performance but also allows students to become active assessors of their own learning.

How to Use This Information

Select a new assessment to try on a regular basis (see Figure 8.5). Keep a journal or other record of how each new assessment works for your students. Take time to share your experiences with colleagues. If your experience with the new activity was positive, your colleagues may want to adopt it in their own classrooms; if not, they may be able to suggest adjustments or alternatives that may work for your students.

3. Interpret formal assessments in context.

When considering the results of formal assessments, which are often inappropriately administered to CLD students (and which cannot be reliably interpreted), teachers must keep certain questions and considerations in mind. The questions in Figure 8.6 provide a starting point for any discussion of standardized-assessment results.

How to Use This Information

As you read through the questions in Figure 8.6, you may find they engender more questions in your mind. To what degree did they impact any one student? Any one assessment? Any one administration of the assessment in your school? You may wish to look at a particular student's file and ask these questions regarding the assessments used to place that student. Not every question will apply to every student, of course. In our experience, however, we found it is likely that one or more of these issues may be relevant to the student and the assessment you consider.

Once you do determine that some of these issues may relate to the assessments which one, several, or all of your students have completed—then what should you do with that information? First, we recommend using it to remind

Figure 8.6	Questions to Consider When Analyzing Assessment Results

- What does the assessment purport to measure?
- Am I using it in a manner that is consistent with that purpose? Or am I trying to gain other information from it?
- Under what circumstances was it given? (At what time of day? In what time frame? At what time of year?)
- Are students familiar with the format of assessment used? Have they had a chance to practice responding to the format used?
- What is the first language (L1) of the students? Are there any linguistic or dialectical issues that might make it difficult for students to access the content of the assessment due to language barriers?
- Who administered the assessment, and did this impact the process or results at all?
- How did the student present, affectively, during the assessment? Were there other factors related to family, outside circumstances, or home situation that might impact the student's performance?
- Was the language of assessment accessible to the student? How do I know? On what evidence am I basing my answer?
- Do the formal assessment results indicated match what you have observed in the classroom? If not, what are the differences?
- Was the student given the opportunity to process information with extended time, if appropriate? If not, how might that have affected the assessment results?
- Was the student provided the opportunity to answer using multiple modalities (e.g., orally, in writing, through art or music, or using drama)? If not, why? How might this have impacted the results of the assessment?
- If the student was asked to respond *only* in writing, or *only* orally, was the assessment measuring writing and language skills, or did it truly measure content knowledge? How do I know this?

yourself that the results of assessments are only one (potentially biased) way of "seeing" students' abilities: For that reason, go out of your way not to prejudge students or preconceive their abilities.

Second, in your future dealings with your students, use your knowledge of students to advocate for appropriate assessment measures whenever you are able to. This may involve advocating for schoolwide adoption of a process based on response to intervention (RTI); it may also involve attending prereferral or intervention team meetings and suggesting a variety of assessments that can help the team arrive at an accurate determination of the student's skills. Finally, you can use this information to inform your own assessment practices.

If you determine your students are not familiar with the format of the districtwide assessments they must take, then you can (if district policy allows) spend time teaching them that format so that they can be more successful. Similarly, if you find that many of your students do not fully understand the language of the assessment, you can ask your department chair or collaborating ESOL teacher whether there are alternative assessments for your students.

SUMMARY

As public school educators know well, assessment is a hot topic these days. However, the purpose and function of assessment, as a whole, is often overlooked; as accountability systems, data tracking, and standardized-test results take precedence over most or all other assessment considerations. While some may see the concept of assessment as being relevant only to high-stakes testing, it must be seen as an essential part of the instructional process, because assessment, when properly conducted, helps to inform and shape the educational process. Teachers considering the relevance of assessment to CLD/E populations must give particular attention to issues of cultural diversity, linguistic diversity, students' prior experience, students' literacy, and students' home situations, among other variables. Each of these has the potential to impact assessment results, creating a strong argument for the integration of informal assessment with formal assessment in order to provide a more accurate picture of each student's abilities.

EXTENSION AND COLLABORATION

1. Survey your colleagues. As a way to begin the conversation on a school-wide level about what assessment practices are used, ask your colleagues some questions about what they do to assess students, both formally and informally. You can share the results with your department chair or administrators to clarify some directions for future staff development. You might survey your colleagues orally or in writing, but whatever method you choose, ask some version of these four important questions to start the conversation:

   a. What informal assessments do you use in the classroom?

   b. On what assessments do your students seem to perform best?

   c. What are the challenges that your students seem to encounter on the assessments used in your classroom?

   d. What questions do you have about assessment in your school?

2. Continue the conversation. Once you have begun this discussion with colleagues, either a small group or the entire staff, you may wish to select one or more areas for ongoing attention in your school improvement plan, staff development training, or even small-group departmental meetings. If none of those options is feasible in your school, find a small group of colleagues with whom you can discuss assessment issues on a regular basis. One suggested practice, easy to implement without much preparation time, is to simply meet once a month to discuss assessment approaches and strategies that are working in your classroom. Ideally, as each member of the group shares successes, others will try new techniques and give more consideration, over time, to issues of cultural and linguistic diversity.

3. Track student performance. In many districts, teachers track student performance on tests, whether they are practice high-stakes assessments or curriculum benchmarks. We suggest that you work with one or two grade-level (or subject-matter) colleagues to also track students' performance on informal assessments, including those discussed in this chapter. You may keep journals of student performance, document grades received in class activities such as skits, or even videotape students (creating, in effect, a digital portfolio

for your students). Make time to discuss your results with colleagues; this may help you to identify assessments that are particularly useful or relevant for your student population.

NEXT STEPS

One of the frequently mentioned solutions to assessment dilemmas involves collaboration. One way to address issues of testing bias is to ensure that students are assessed (and decisions about placement, instruction, and service delivery are made) through a collaborative process where several educators have input, the students' abilities can be seen from multiple perspectives, and assessments in multiple formats can be used to provide a comprehensive view of strengths, challenges, and ongoing needs. Accordingly, we believe the best way to follow a discussion of assessment is with a discussion of collaboration, because collaborative skills are needed to complete a holistic and student-centered assessment process. Collaborative skills are also needed to implement whatever decisions an assessment team might reach. As you read Chapter 9, consider the ways in which the ability to collaborate can enrich both your assessment and your instructional practice.

COMMUNITY CONNECTIONS

1. Communicate with family members. The law requires schools to communicate with families about each school's assessments and their impact on AYP. However, the law does not necessarily mandate that schools go out of their way to make information available in multiple formats, to present it in family friendly language, and to actively solicit families' input on the assessment process. Suggest one or more of these steps at your next staff meeting, or even better, volunteer to hold a meeting or draft a communication to families that can serve as the first step in this process.

2. Consider looking within the community for assessment ideas. Older students can complete community-based projects for language arts, social studies, or science classes; younger students can research a building, office, or organization in their community and share information about it in class (through written work, oral discussion, drawing, or a diorama).

USEFUL WEBSITES

- Center for Applied Special Technology: www.cast.org. CAST is a nonprofit organization that specializes in research related to universal design for learning (UDL) and accessibility. While the CAST website does not focus specifically on assessment, we highly recommend it as a background resource that can enrich the way in which you design and structure your assessments for inclusive teaching.

- Discovery Education: http://school.discoveryeducation.com/schrockguide/ assess.html. This site, compiled by Kathy Schrock, contains a wealth of information, particularly in relation to portfolio assessment and rubrics. The site contains sample assessment rubrics and templates, overviews of the various types of assessment, and strategies for implementation.
- National Alternate Assessment Center: www.naacpartners.org. This website, funded by a five-year grant from the U.S. Department of Education, disseminates the work of the NAAC. Much of the site provides research related to large-scale, standardized, and alternate assessments and provides important background to considerations related to testing validity.
- National Capital Language Resource Center: www.nclrc.org/portfolio/ modules.html. This site, compiled by the NCLRC, provides an overview of the theory and issues related to portfolio implementation. While some of the information provided is specific to foreign-language instruction, it is also relevant to second-language learning and to general education as well.

9 Collaboration
Working Together for Student Success

Francisco was an outgoing and cheerful student, one who loved to laugh and tell jokes with his third-grade peers. Ms. Rivers, his classroom teacher, had become increasingly concerned about his academic skills and his progress. She requested a meeting of the ESOL (English for speakers of other languages) teacher, counselor, reading specialist, and resource room teacher so that they could identify the source of his difficulties and decide upon some potential interventions. The school had recently moved to a collaborative-intervention framework, and Ms. Rivers felt some trepidation about how this new program would impact Francisco. As the meeting progressed, though, she felt greatly relieved. The team had reviewed Francisco's work and progress to date, identified some specific challenges in the area of reading comprehension and math problem solving, and constructed specific interventions that could be implemented in the general education setting. A plan was developed to track the effectiveness of each intervention, and the team agreed to meet again in two weeks to follow up. As she left, Ms. Rivers breathed a sigh of relief. "That," she said to herself, "is how the process is supposed to work! Let's just hope it keeps working for the next two weeks!"

THE ISSUES

- Identification of students' needs
- Definition of *collaboration*
- Collaboration to improve student outcomes
- Establishing structures and procedures for successful collaboration (steps involved in successful collaboration)
- Follow-up, evaluation of collaborative efforts, and monitoring to ensure continued success

QUESTIONS TO CONSIDER

1. How does the team share information to determine what support might best meet Francisco's needs?

2. What concerns does Ms. Rivers bring to the table, and how does the team use an interdisciplinary approach to solve them?

3. What steps are involved?

4. What potential challenges or pitfalls might the team encounter in the next two weeks that may make it more difficult to have a positive outcome?

GETTING THE ANSWERS

What is collaboration?

Collaboration is a frequently used term, in fact almost a buzzword, in many schools settings today. Districts offer collaborative courses; schools have adopted collaborative-planning periods and problem-solving approaches for teams, and individual classrooms teachers are encouraged to collaborate with colleagues whenever possible.

There are numerous definitions of collaboration. However, for our purposes, we define collaboration as a process by which stakeholders can come together for a common purpose to exchange information, listen to one another's experiences and perspectives, and work together toward a common goal. The goal is generally one that cannot be reached without the input of all participants, so each person's participation in the process is essential to the success of the entire project. Collaboration must not only be multidisciplinary but must be grounded in a transdisciplinary outlook (Godemann, 2008). In other words, the process is not only *multidisciplinary*, involving participants from various disciplines, but *transdisciplinary*, meaning that participants provide their expertise, as part of the process, but also work to transcend the potential biases and preconceptions that they may have as a function of their training and role. This process, sometimes also known as "role release," is an important element of success, as the ability to generate new solutions involves creating a climate in which participants can listen to one another and embrace ideas that different members suggest.

True collaboration creates a climate in which individuals can bring their diverse sets of knowledge, expertise, perceptions, and ideas, so the process is no longer static but involves individuals exchanging knowledge. Collaboration challenges individuals to rethink their own perceptions and consider alternatives, with the result that the process is dynamic and can allow each participant to rethink beliefs, biases, and approaches based on interactions with other members of the team.

What is the purpose of collaboration?

The purpose of collaboration in the educational setting is most often to improve educational outcomes for students. Improving student outcomes can take a variety of forms: collaboration to improve student achievement, to improve assessment and referral procedures, to support the development of specific behaviors, to provide professional development for school staff, to increase family outreach and involvement, or to engage the community in supporting the school.

Each of these endeavors or activities may seem quite different from the next. However, when they are undertaken in a collaborative manner, they share certain characteristics. In a truly collaborative process, individuals do not leave the table to pursue their own goals in isolation from each other. Rather, they share their beliefs and leave with a common goal, able to move toward an outcome that is agreed upon and, also, able to identify a process by which to work toward that goal.

Collaboration also involves a philosophical component. Participants must believe strongly that "the whole is greater than the sum of its parts": In other words, they must believe that the process will be of benefit to them. Participants must believe not only that they have something to contribute but also that they have something to learn from each person around the table. Principals and school leaders can force teachers to have meetings, but they cannot force the spirit of collaboration—this must originate within the group as a shared commitment on the part of each participant.

In addition to depending on a shared outlook and belief, collaboration requires teacher "buy-in." It is a challenge to require teachers to collaborate when they are already busy with numerous other classroom duties. One school superintendent, for example, found himself in a battle with his city's teachers union after he added a requirement for a 45-minute weekly collaboration period to the teachers' week (Neufeld, 2009). Clearly, a mandate alone is not enough to force collaboration. Rather, collaboration requires a set of common dispositions, mutual confidence, trust, and availability. Also, teachers need a wide repertoire of academic, linguistic, and interpersonal skills so that the onus for learning does not fall on categorical groups of students, be they labeled according to their gender, their ethnicity, their cultural background, their language background and status, or any other definition of *difference* that we might construct. The process of gaining these skills begins with reflection: How can you know what skills you need if you don't know what skills you have? What skills your students need? What strategies and approaches are most effective for them?

What are the implications of collaborative planning and intervention?

In other words, what is to be gained from using a collaborative process? First of all, collaboration makes it possible for each collaborator to be impacted positively by others at the table. Through collaboration, viewpoints are exchanged and different ideas are shared.

Collaboration also offers a powerful way to shape interventions with input from all who might be able to contribute. Culturally and linguistically diverse exceptional (CLD/E) students' needs are often best met through collaboration, as no one practitioner at the table possesses the sum total of knowledge needed to appropriately support the student. In the scenario at the start of the chapter, Ms. Rivera, the classroom teacher, appreciated this fact when she called a meeting that included all of these personnel.

Especially as demographics shift and pressure on teachers rises in the wake of NCLB (No Child Left Behind), educators are increasingly confronted with the question of how to separate difference from disability. How do we tell the difference between a child in the process of second-language acquisition and a child with a genuine disability? And how do culture and language influence the assessment process? New initiatives such as RTI (response to intervention) offer the potential to sidestep traditional concerns regarding assessment and special education eligibility through a multidisciplinary process that is focused on designing appropriate interventions and monitoring the student's progress, rather than on waiting for the child to fail and then administering static, standardized assessments to determine a supposed need for extra support (VanDerHeyden, 2008). RTI, which was incorporated into the revised IDEA 2004 as a legally permissible alternative to the "discrepancy" model for special education eligibility determination, provides a way to identify students' areas of difficulty, immediately provide targeted intervention to address those needs, and monitor the intervention over time in order to increase the intensity of support if necessary. If additional support does not seem to have an impact on the student's performance, as measured by the data collected through progress monitoring, then the student can be considered for special education services.

RTI appears to be a promising approach to reduce problems such as disproportionate identification of minorities and CLD students for special education service (Xu & Drame, 2008). By providing immediate intervention, it has potential to reduce the gap between the period when the student's needs are identified and eligibility is determined, thereby qualifying the student for services. Numerous school systems throughout the United States have moved toward adopting RTI-based practices in at least some of their schools (Xu & Drame, 2008). In this approach, schools use "tiered interventions" (VanDerHeyden, 2008) to meet a child's needs. If an intervention is not successful, the child is moved up to a more intensive tier, with the final tier being placement in special education (VanDerHeyden, Witt, & Gilbertson, 2007). First-tier and sometimes second-tier interventions are typically implemented in the general education setting and are most often the responsibility of the classroom teacher. Third-tier and, where applicable, fourth-tier interventions are often implemented with consistent support from specialists, whether they take place in the general education setting or in a pullout setting.

Even more than traditional interventions, which might be designed and implemented solely by a classroom teacher, RTI depends on collaboration to work properly. Interventions are often designed by a team of educators, using expertise from each; so the input of specialists (special education teachers, ESOL teachers, counselors, pupil personnel workers, and so on) is essential to the task. However, the classroom teacher plays a crucial role in implementing the first and second tier of interventions and in collecting the data to analyze their effectiveness. For this reason, RTI requires that specialists and general educators be in constant communication, so implementation, data collection, and progress monitoring can be carried out with input from all parties.

What does collaboration look like in practice?

Collaboration can occur in any model, though some models (dual-immersion, inclusion of special education students, and coteaching, for example) and some new practices, such as RTI, might more easily support collaborative practice by placing teachers from different roles together to plan, implement, and monitor instruction and interventions in any number of settings (Johnson, Mellard, Fuchs, & McKnight, 2006). Even in that case, however, the dispositions and availability of the teachers involved can be as important to the success of collaborative efforts as any other factor. We have been in classrooms, for example, where coteaching and coplanning models are in place, but the special educator assigned to an inclusive content-area classroom functions much as a paraeducator would, circulating to support individual students rather than sharing instructional responsibility for the entire class with the content teacher.

This process can include elements such as strategies for classroom management, strategies for behavior management, continued review of interventions to ensure they are meeting students' needs, ongoing adjustment as needed based on input from all participants, and formative and summative evaluation.

Let's take a look at how a truly collaborative process might differ from that in which varying professionals all remain on their own page, state their own stance and perspective, and are not willing to accommodate their ideas to others. Consider the ideas presented in the scenarios in Figure 9.1. As you read and respond to the reflection questions that follow, list your ideas about what made the process work—or not—in each case. Consider the ways in which school staff interacted, the goals of the process, the perspectives that each participant brought to the process, and the way in which the process was facilitated.

| **Figure 9.1** | Collaboration in Practice: Two Approaches |

Approach 1

Shirese is a new student at Kingston Middle School whose family has lived in the United States for some time. He has been academically successful and, as his family has lived in the United States for some time, considers himself to be a "real American," a phrase that he frequently repeated in conversations with his friends. He has been exited from ESOL. While his academic achievement is still meeting expectations, Shirese has been in four fights over the past three weeks. His teachers have sent him to the office six times over the past month, and his teachers have assessed numerous in-class consequences against him. His classroom teacher has suggested that his teachers get together for a discussion.

In the first scenario, Shirese's teachers each discuss their varying views and then reach some conclusions:

"I'm glad we discussed it," said his language arts teacher. "I had no idea that was happening in my class."

The math teacher said, "Well, in my class, I really can't change the rules. You need to sit down and be quiet and do your work. I can't let him sit down and not do work if I make all the other students do it."

The English teacher said, "I can give him some positive behavioral support. . . . I have positive-reinforcement stamps I give out that he can use at the school store if he has a good day. I can give the rest of you some stamps if you want to use them too."

The social studies teacher said, "Thanks, but I don't actually use stamps. However, I think we may also need input from the guidance office. I am not sure what his problem is, but it seems like there are some underlying issues for sure." As the conference concluded, the teachers determined they would refer Shirese to the guidance counselor. The math teacher also decided to take some stamps from the English teacher to try to reinforce positive behavior. The math and English teachers determined that, for each day Shirese avoided getting into any fights, he would get a card. Ten cards would allow him to buy a small item at the school store.

(Continued)

Figure 9.1 (Continued)

Approach 2

In the second scenario, Shirese's teachers opened by asking, "Do we know of anything in his home or family situation that has changed?" His teachers began by brainstorming about Shirese's current and past behavior in school. The algebra teacher pointed out, after thinking for a few minutes, that his older brother used to pick him up from school but had not been seen in some time. The next day, the language arts teacher casually mentioned Shirese's older brother to him and found out his brother had returned to their native country to see the rest of their extended family. The language arts teacher suggested that Shirese see the guidance counselor but also asked the math teacher, who spoke the native language of the family, to translate on a phone call to Shirese's family members. While the conversation was not long, Shirese's aunt, who answered the phone, indicated that she appreciated the call. The teachers made sure to make positive comments about Shirese, hoping to build his sense of security at school, and were gratified to see that he returned to school the next morning with a small smile on his face.

The teachers shared information over the next two days in order to identify what Shirese seemed to find most motivating, and constructed a behavioral incentive system that rewarded him with small credits at the school store, where he could purchase needed school supplies. Over time, Shirese's attitude and completion of work seemed to improve, and his teachers continued to meet monthly, for the next four months, to monitor his progress.

As you reflect on the two examples in Figure 9.1, ask yourself (or a colleague) some of the following questions:

- What differences do you notice in the ways that the teachers approached Shirese's progress?
- What questions were asked in each scenario? How did those questions lead to different answers?
- What interventions were tried first? Second? Third? In each scenario? Which order seemed to be more effective? Which order would you try if you were in the situation?
- How did the teachers work together to identify the problem and develop solutions? At what points did collaboration—or the lack of it—significantly impact the process?

Reflecting on these questions can be a valuable exercise (particularly if completed prior to assessing your own collaborative practices, school environment, and collaborative goals). The following activities will help you do just that.

NEW STEPS TO TAKE—TOMORROW

This manual is written primarily for teachers. If we had set out to write a handbook for administrators, this would be the appropriate place to discuss systemwide strategies to support collaboration, professional development that could be implemented buildingwide, and other strategies to support

Collaboration can strengthen relationships among teachers while also allowing them to communicate about students' progress and plan instruction and interventions together.

development of a collaborative culture within a building or district. All of these are tremendously important to the development of a collaborative approach to service delivery. However, we recognize that, as a classroom teacher, your ability to effect change in these arenas, no matter how important they are, may be limited—at least in the immediate future. Over time, as you share your ideas with colleagues and administrators, you may find that you are able to make more of an impact than one might initially anticipate. For the immediate future, though, we believe it appropriate to focus on those things that do lie indisputably within your control: your knowledge, your practices, and your interactions with others.

Accordingly, then, we have structured this section somewhat differently from the way in which it has been structured in previous chapters. We do still encourage you to begin the process of reflection tomorrow (or even today). However, your final "product" will be, not an activity that you complete but, a set of goals that you set for yourself in regard to collaboration.

1. Evaluate your own practices with regard to collaboration.

In Figure 9.2, we listed some common behaviors and attitudes that are often indicative of the existence of collaborative practices. We encourage

Figure 9.2 Collaborative Practices Checklist

Directions: Place a check on the line ("Yes" or "No") that best describes your response to the question. If you would like to note comments for your own use (including ways to change the situation or behaviors described in the question, or reflections on specific factors that might have influenced your collaborative habits), use the comment area that follows each question.

1. I believe that teachers should make time to communicate with one another about ongoing instruction, assessment, and student success in their classrooms.
   _____ Yes   _____ No   Comments:

2. I believe that teachers in the same grade level, department, or subject area should make time to plan lessons together and to share feedback about students' success on the lessons.
   _____ Yes   _____ No   Comments:

3. I believe most teachers would collaborate more frequently if given more "collaborative planning time" by school or district rules.
   _____ Yes   _____ No   Comments:

4. I believe collaboration among teachers can have a direct impact on student achievement.
   _____ Yes   _____ No   Comments:

5. I believe collaborative planning is one of the most important activities teachers can complete.
   _____ Yes   _____ No   Comments:

6. Within the last year, I have asked a colleague to work with me to plan an instructional or behavioral program for a student.
   _____ Yes   _____ No   Comments:

7. When requested by a colleague, I have discussed a student's strengths and needs in order to collaboratively plan for that student's educational program.
   _____ Yes   _____ No   Comments:

8. Within the last year, I have asked a colleague to sit down with me to discuss a student's strengths and needs in order to collaboratively plan for that student's educational program.
   _____ Yes   _____ No   Comments:

9. Within the last year, I have invited and scheduled time for the families of the students in my class to share their insights about their child with me on a scheduled basis.
   _____ Yes   _____ No   Comments:

10. Within the past year, I have discussed my lessons with my school's parent liaison or family coordinator, with the pupil personnel worker, and with counselors, where appropriate, to determine how students' social, socioeconomic, and emotional situations may impact or be impacted by my instruction.
    _____ Yes   _____ No   Comments:

11. I meet weekly or monthly with my collaborating special education teacher (or if you are the special education teacher, with the general education or ESOL teacher) to exchange feedback and suggestions about the progress of my students with special education needs.
    _____ Yes   _____ No   Comments:

12. I meet weekly or monthly with my collaborating ESOL teacher (or if you are the ESOL teacher, with the general education or special education teacher) to exchange feedback and suggestions about the progress of my students who are second-language learners.
    _____ Yes   _____ No   Comments:

13. I spend time at least once a week in another teacher's classroom for the purpose of observing instruction, supporting instruction, or observing assessment.
    _____ Yes   _____ No   Comments:

14. I ask my students for feedback about my lessons and share the feedback with my team members at least once a month.
    _____ Yes   _____ No   Comments:

15. I share strategies, suggestions, or questions with my department chair or other administrators at least once a month to better address approaches or issues that may impact the success of my students and others in the school.
    _____ Yes   _____ No   Comments:

you to review this checklist and assess your own behaviors and dispositions in regard to collaborating with colleagues. Next to each item, you'll notice there is also a space to indicate potential ways to change the behavior or disposition, if your answer indicates a lack of collaborative practices or skills. This is your space to think and brainstorm—there are no right or wrong answers, and you will gain the most benefit from the checklist if you answer it honestly.

How to Use This Information

As you may have noticed, some of the items in Figure 9.2 may apply to everyone; some may not apply to you. Mark the answer that you feel is most accurate—your responses are visible to nobody except yourself. Use the space in the comments column to identify areas you wish to improve or change, or to note a particular situation that has been challenging for you.

After you finish the self-assessment, take some time to review your answers. Consider the comments that you wrote; or if you did not write any comments when you first took the survey, take time to think about some now. What factors have influenced your collaborative practices? What makes it easy or difficult for you to collaborate? Which habits and practices, if any, would you like to change? This may be a useful lead-in to Number 2 and Number 3, which ask you to identify elements in your school that facilitate collaboration and then set goals for yourself.

2. Identify elements in your school that facilitate collaboration.

Some schools, particularly as they move toward adopting collaborative-intervention models such as RTI, have undertaken a process to increase the support available for teacher collaboration. It is helpful to take stock of the elements or structures already in place in your school that can facilitate the process of collaboration. Doing so may help you to recognize some existing processes, structures, or opportunities that are already in place; or it may help you identify one or more elements that you could ask your administrators to include in future years (or you could work with colleagues to facilitate that goal).

How to Use This Information

The chart in Figure 9.3 may seem to reiterate information you already know. However, it is more than possible that you have not had the opportunity to consider all of these factors together—or to consider the ways in which they may impact your availability to collaborate. For each item that you marked "Yes," ask yourself how you can use this resource or this support to collaborate more effectively. For items that you marked "No," consider working with colleagues, or approaching administrators, to discuss ways to open the door to collaborative practice.

Figure 9.3   Elements in My School That Can Facilitate Collaboration

Indicator of Frameworks for Collaboration	Yes	No
Staff have daily planning periods and can meet with colleagues during this time.		
Planning periods are scheduled so that teachers within the same department or grade level have the same planning periods.		
Peer observations (colleague to colleague) are possible and even encouraged.		
Teachers are encouraged to contact families frequently with positive as well as constructive feedback.		
Family events are planned each semester or more frequently and allow families and teachers the chance to exchange meaningful information about students.		
Prereferral team meetings include a variety of teachers in a variety of roles.		
Teachers are able to communicate with one another in a variety of ways (face-to-face, e-mail, phone, or regularly scheduled planning periods).		
Teachers are able to communicate with administrators in a variety of ways (face-to-face, e-mail, phone, or regularly scheduled meeting times).		

Before school or during lunch can sometimes be the most convenient time to meet with colleagues and plan together.

3. Set collaborative goals for yourself.

After considering your current practices, your knowledge of practices that facilitate collaboration, and the resources available in your school; you are now ready to set goals for your own collaborative practices. Your goals may cover any of the areas in Figure 9.4 or additional ones that you identify.

How to Use This Information

Your goals for collaborative practice should draw upon the information you listed in the previous two activities (see Figures 9.2 and 9.3). Consider the practices in which you currently engage; and consider, also, your school climate and needs. Based on these two factors, you should be able to identify one or more goals for the remainder of the school year with respect to collaboration. Perhaps you could return to one of the items, in Figure 9.2, that you marked "No." Consider the comments you wrote next to the item and formulate a measurable goal that can help you achieve that behavior or step. In the same way, examine the practices and resources that currently exist in your school (see Figure 9.3), and as an alternative to the first suggestion, consider making one of those practices your own personal goal. You could work with administrators, for example, to increase opportunities for teacher collaborative planning through scheduling; you could work with colleagues to conduct staff development about the need for collaboration and the value of collaborative planning (as well as training in effective collaboration skills). Most of all, the goals you set should be useful and relevant to you, in your own classroom and school situation.

Figure 9.4   My Collaborative Goals

Facilitating Communication Practices

Coplanning

Coteaching and Sharing Instructional Responsibility

Ongoing Monitoring and Providing Feedback to Colleagues

Communicating With Others Within the School Building

Seeking Opportunities to Communicate With Families

Addressing Challenges

SUMMARY

Collaboration is, fortunately, increasingly being recognized as one of the most important aspects of a successfully functioning educational system. This chapter reviewed the rationale for collaboration, presented some strategies and suggestions for collaborating, and provided an overview of collaborative (as opposed to noncollaborative) approaches to student success. The chapter then provided some tools that you can use to assess your own collaborative practices, take stock of your school's procedures with respect to collaboration, and formulate personal goals for collaboration throughout the year.

EXTENSION AND COLLABORATION

1. Research additional resources. An Internet search of terms such as "collaboration checklist" will turn up a wealth of self-assessments and lists, each detailing elements of the collaborative process that may differ from the ones presented here. Select one or two, and present them, along with the checklist provided in Figure 9.2, to your colleagues. Ask them to identify the checklist item that they think most "captures" the behaviors and traits associated with effective collaboration. You may find that the ensuing discussion is useful in providing time and space for each of you to clarify your own ideas and expectations.

2. Ask for feedback. One of the hardest things to do, in our experience, is to ask a colleague and peer for honest feedback. Think back and select a situation in which you interacted with a colleague to solve a challenge or problem. (Perhaps you attempted to solve it but were not successful.) Approach your colleague at a convenient time, when you have the opportunity for honest conversation (not in the lunch line!), and ask him or her to share some thoughts about your own performance in that situation. Were you an effective collaborator? Which of your actions helped to facilitate the collaborative process? Which did not? It is not always easy to hear feedback, particularly if your colleague openly shares concerns or reservations with your behavior during the process. Keep in mind that doing so is a necessary part of the process and can help you to become a more effective collaborator. You may want to review the feedback and revisit the goals you set for yourself earlier in the chapter.

3. Share with a wider audience. Ask your principal if you can share the collaborative practices checklist from Figure 9.2 at a staff meeting. You do not need to review each item, but you may want to select one or two to briefly discuss; or ask colleagues to look at the checklist and select concepts they see as important for future discussion.

NEXT STEPS

Considering the value of collaboration (and seeking ways to maximize collaborative attitudes and behaviors) is a natural lead-in to the topic of family involvement.

We often think of collaboration, in the school setting, as an activity involving teachers working with teachers—or teachers working with administrators, school counselors, or other school-based personnel. We forget, sometimes, that among the most important collaborative relationships we can have is the relationship that educators have with their students' families. Knowing students' backgrounds, valuing their heritage, understanding their culture and language, and learning about their families' hopes, goals, and resources all can help teachers to serve these students more effectively. As you read the final chapter, on family involvement, think back to some of the ideas raised in this chapter. Challenge yourself to identify new ways of reaching out to families and bringing them into the school setting, not as observers or listeners but as true collaborators who can help to shape the direction of your instruction.

COMMUNITY CONNECTIONS

1. Though it is addressed more extensively in Chapter 10, communication and collaboration with families is an important aspect of collaboration in general. Work with your school's family outreach coordinator to identify ways that your school can build collaborative communication and relationships with families.

2. Identify one or more schools in your community with which you have common interests. You might have similar student populations, neighborhoods, histories, or faculty profiles. Contact one of the school staff members to determine whether it might be helpful for you to plan events together, exchange information, or share resources in order to better support staff and students at both schools.

USEFUL WEBSITES

- ASCD: www.ascd.org. ASCD is one of the leading curriculum and instruction organizations in the United States. Their website contains a number of useful resources on collaboration, team teaching, and coplanning.
- RTI Action Network: www.rtinetwork.org. The RTI Action Network, composed of a number of collaborating organizations to provide information and support related to implementation of RTI, has resources on its website to support collaborative planning, collaborative interventions, and progress monitoring—particularly within the framework of tiered interventions such as RTI.

10 Family Involvement

Forming Rich and Lasting Partnerships

Mayana sighed. She had wiped off each desk in her brightly decorated first-grade classroom; she had hung up her students' most recent artwork and labeled each desk with a student's name; she had taped a "Welcome to 1A" sign to her door. She had even put out juice, water, coffee, and cookies on the table where she usually held small-group reading activities. And with all of that effort, she had a total of three parents show up to Back-to-School Night. As she took down the welcome sign and bagged up the cookies to bring down to the teachers' lounge, the thought crossed her mind: "I put a lot of effort into getting ready for this. Maybe I should have put some of that effort into contacting the parents!"

THE ISSUES

- Need for increased family involvement in schools
- Need for teachers and administrators to involve families
- Policies to maximize family involvement
- Communication among families, schools, and community organizations

QUESTIONS TO CONSIDER

1. What are the benefits, and the barriers or challenges, to families' involvement in the educational process?

2. As Mayana recognized, she spent a great deal more time preparing her classroom than she spent reaching out to the families of her students. How might she have increased her outreach to family members?

3. How might Mayana's school rethink its back-to-school night to foster increased involvement for families?

4. How could Mayana and her school administrators partner with community organizations to involve and support families and students?

GETTING THE ANSWERS

We tend to think of students in the school setting as entities in and of themselves, as learners who exist primarily in relationship to their teachers and peers. However, students bring with them, each day, the experiences they have had at home. Each of these experiences impacts a student's availability to learn, personal values, approach to school and learning, and self-concept. Many counselors, psychologists, and educators subscribe to a theory called the *family systems approach.* This approach is far more complex than we are able to describe within this book, but briefly, family systems theory (sometimes referred to as Bowen family systems theory, after the psychologist who developed it) holds that a family is its own system, in which each family member has specific roles and activities that relate to the functioning of the system as a whole. As a result, students (and family members) must be viewed within the context of the overall family system in order to gain an accurate picture of their status, role, and relationships at home (Nichols & Schwartz, 2004). Viewed within this context, students are not just independent individuals functioning in the classroom. Rather, each student assumes particular relationships, roles, and attitudes as a result of family dynamics, and understanding those dynamics is an important part of understanding one's students. For this reason, teachers and administrators can gain greatly from learning about their students' family dynamics, relationships, and circumstances. School personnel can reach out to families to learn more about students; they can also invite families to share information about what motivates their children, how their children learn, and what family experiences might be relevant to the child's educational progress (Epstein & Sanders, 2000).

This theoretical benefit translates into solid academic and social gains for students whose families are involved in the educational process and whose families have a strong relationship with schools. Research is clear about the value of family involvement, particularly for diverse learners. Family involvement has been shown to increase student outcomes in a variety of areas: attendance, behavior, academic skills and achievement, and positive relationships with school staff (Henderson & Mapp, 2002; Henderson & Berla, 1994; Sheldon, 2003).

Educators must keep in mind, also, that the relationship between schools and families is a mutually beneficial one. Just as students and families benefit from increased parental (or familial) involvement (Henderson & Mapp, 2002; Snow, Barnes, Chandler, Goodman, & Hemphill, 1991), schools can also benefit from involvement of all their parents (Sheldon, 2003; Downey, 2002). Diverse families can contribute information about their own rich heritage, experience, cultures, beliefs, and traditions; enriching the ongoing conversation within the school and providing teachers with information that can help

Teachers can ensure students' family members feel valued as partners by scheduling meetings at convenient times, allowing family members to view students' work posted in the classroom, and opening the meeting with a discussion of families' hopes and goals for their student.

to establish rapport with diverse learners, improving instruction while strengthening the socioemotional value of the educational experience. Curriculum, instruction, and assessment can all be enriched by the addition of diverse perspectives and backgrounds, which may not have been considered in the original planning of instruction. The linguistic diversity that many parents bring with them can further enrich the linguistic diversity of the school—as well as provide students with exposure to new languages and cultures. Families from cultures that traditionally have strong extended-family relationships have much to contribute; the presence of grandparents, aunts, uncles, and cousins can provide ongoing support to students and, in close-knit neighborhoods, can provide a network of informal support for other students as well. Furthermore, families can help to suggest new and innovative ways to involve members of the community and to connect with community organizations or institutions that may be important in the lives of students.

The realities of life can create stressors that may impact family schedules and availability. These challenges can include any of the following: socioeconomic stress (which may necessitate working multiple jobs, taking shift jobs, or not being able to afford child care for younger children); differing cultural experiences and perceptions of the relationship between home and school; linguistic accessibility of the school community for parents who use English as a second language (ESL); differing cultural experiences and perceptions regarding the nature of the American school experience; and fear of being deported upon becoming "known" to school administrators. This list is not by any means exhaustive; as you consider the families in your own school and community, you may find yourself identifying more barriers still. Each of these can have its own impact on family involvement, as we typically define it, in that such factors can contribute to driving down parent attendance rates at events like the traditional back-to-school night.

As with many issues involving CLD students, increasing family involvement, for school staff, is often a matter of adjusting one's lens rather than reflexively blaming families for not being more involved. As with students' learning, there is a continuum of involvement and communication for families. The mother who, for whatever reasons, does not attend a PTA meeting may nevertheless make a habit of asking her child, every day, how his school day was, what he learned, and who he played with. President Barack Obama (2009) provided a striking model of such parental involvement in his 2009 address to schoolchildren, when he told a story of his mother waking him up at 4:30 each morning to study before school. Whether or not his mother, or others like her, attended PTA meetings may be beside the point. Rather than focusing on what parents did not do ("I can't believe she hasn't come to any meetings this year!"), teachers must instead focus on the support families do provide and the very real sense of commitment and partnership that many families exhibit through their day-to-day activities: talking to their children about school, purchasing school supplies, setting up study space in a one-room apartment, waking the child up for school, and talking about their own school experiences.

If families face child-care pressures, schools can consider providing child care for events, or making it clear, in flyers and announcements, that siblings and other family members are welcome. Further steps to make it clear that families are welcome might include any of the following: providing food for families who would otherwise have to skip their dinner hour; providing or coordinating transportation; "buddying" ELL parents with those who have more English proficiency; and matching up new families with those who have been at the school longer in another twist on the buddy system.

If families in the school community have not had the opportunity to build trusting relationships with educators, teachers and administrators can attend community events or take other steps to build their presence in the community and among families. If language is a barrier to communication, schools can often access interpreters and translation assistance via their central office. Principals can also use their hiring opportunities to prioritize bilingual staff members or those familiar with the cultural background of the community and school.

Students can learn from their families' educational and life experiences.

As Mayana thought, in the opening vignette, effectively solving the challenge of family involvement requires, first, thinking critically about what efforts have already been made, what the needs of the community and the school's families really are, what issues or circumstances might prevent their involvement, and what changes may need to be made to current outreach efforts.

NEW STEPS TO TAKE—TOMORROW

1. Rethink the concept of "family involvement."

We frequently think of family involvement as a one-way exchange of information. In this view, families passively receive information from teachers and administrators and adjust their family routines and activities to support the needs of the school and of their child. (Adding time for homework, reading aloud, and extracurricular activities is one potential adjustment that might be made.) If families are asked to share information, it is often restricted to that which is most relevant to their child's immediate instructional needs: "Does Rosina enjoy having someone read stories to her?" Rather than embrace this somewhat colonialist model (in which the school "authority" tells others what to do and how to do it), we subscribe to a view of family involvement that is rooted in theories of cultural responsiveness and in which families have much to contribute to the life of the school. Family traditions, alternative or unfamiliar belief systems that suggest a different way of viewing the world (or school, or students), and new understandings of language and communication: All of these are areas in which families' differences from the "norm" or the prevailing school culture can be a source of richness and strength for all in the school. As administrators, teachers, and other students become familiar with one another's diverse cultural backgrounds, the school community has an excellent chance not only to grow in tolerance but also, potentially, to learn new practices, approaches, and beliefs that may help to reach students from diverse backgrounds.

There are numerous areas where families may wish to be involved but may feel uncomfortable attending events due to financial, child-care, or other concerns (including immigration policy). In this case, revise your expectations for the events. Rather than focusing on the families who did not attend, take the opportunity to enjoy and appreciate the chance for a more intimate, and less hurried, conversation with those who do attend. Rather than seeing "parents' night" as the be-all-end-all of communication with your students' families, consider it as one of many opportunities to communicate with families, which will allow you to create a special and more personal interaction with those families who are able to participate in this particular activity.

Also, consider what type of event is most likely to appeal to families. As Mayana found out in the vignette opening up this chapter, the most meticulously prepared parents' night is not worthwhile if few parents come to it. If family members are unable to participate in events or activities, consider adding other avenues for communication with families and supporting a more diverse view of family involvement. Your students' family members and students themselves may be the best sources of information regarding events, activities, and programs that would be useful, feasible for them to attend, and would help them feel valued as partners in their children's education.

How to Use This Information

When you rethink your beliefs and perhaps even your biases, you may discover that your view of family involvement changes in accord with new insights about your students and your community—or about your school's practices. The process of "rethinking" these ideas is one that is gradual—and so you may find yourself putting your revised beliefs into practice in any number of ways. You may approach a colleague or administrator to discuss additional ways for your school to reach out to families; you may restructure some of your classroom practices to acknowledge the realities under which parents and students function each day. For example, you may revise the hours and the locations you are available to conference with families, or you may find alternative media for reaching out to families (including notes, attending community events, electronic media, or student assignments that could ask students to report on family traditions or important family moments). In the sections that follow, you will find additional ideas for putting your beliefs into practice and encouraging school-based colleagues to do the same.

2. Evaluate the breadth and accessibility of your school's communication with families.

Figure 10.1 provides a list of the areas in which schools may need to communicate with families throughout the year—providing information to families and soliciting information from families. For each of these items, reflect on whether parents are provided information regarding the area and, if so, whether the information is linguistically accessible. Is it given in written as well as oral form? Are parents provided a chart or graphic organizer to make important school-related info memorable and easy to access? This table provides a handy way to look across categories and concepts to verify that meaningful connections have been made. Review the list, checking for areas where your school might strengthen the amount or frequency of its communications with families.

How to Use This Information

You may find that your school's communications with parents are already well developed and incorporate elements that are useful for parents from a variety of cultural and linguistic backgrounds. If not, use this list (see Figure 10.1) as a sort of checklist or self-assessment. For each area in the list, ask yourself (or facilitate a nonthreatening conversation with administrators in order to ask them) some of the following questions as appropriate:

- Are materials provided in languages that are accessible to all of the school's cultural and linguistic groups?

Figure 10.1 Areas of Two-Way Communication Between Schools and Families

Areas of Communication From Schools to Families

Has our school done everything we can to share information with families in the following areas?

Topic or Area	Yes	No
School routines		
Emergency procedures		
Health policies and requirements		
School policies		
Academic demands and expectations		
Social activities or extracurricular activities before or after school		
HSA (Home and School Association) activities and involvement		

Areas of Communication From Families to Schools

Has our school done everything we can to solicit our families' input in the following areas?

Topic or Area	Yes	No
School policies and rules		
Means of communicating with families about emergency and health policies		
Methods of involving families		
Opportunities for communication among schools and families		
Academic demands and support provided to students		
Social activities or extracurricular opportunities available to students		
HSA (Home and School Association) activities and involvement		

- Are materials disseminated through multiple modalities: in-person announcements, automatic calls, flyers and letters, and signs posted in the schools?
- Are families provided an opportunity to ask questions about the topic or topics?
- Are families provided an opportunity to give input into what topics or issues they would like to see addressed?
- In areas where schools can be flexible according to family needs and circumstances (homework policies, for example, or preferred methods of communication), does the school communicate that parent and family feedback is welcome?
- Are families aware of the distinct areas where communication is expected or required?
- Are families aware of the different avenues to communicate with school personnel (face-to-face visits, phone, and e-mail) and how to use each? Are school personnel open to parent communication in each of these forms?
- Is information accessible linguistically, provided in multiple languages and with content "sheltered" (simplified and reinforced with visuals) for CLD families?

If you can answer yes to each of these questions, then you are ready to check the "Yes" box in the chart. If not, consider your family outreach a work in progress, and identify one or more areas to improve each month or semester.

3. Get to know your school's parents and family members.

Figure 10.2 and Figure 10.3 illustrate two examples of surveys that can be used to gain information from family members. Each has a slightly different purpose: The first survey is designed to gain information about the student, the student's skills, the family's expectations regarding school, and the ways in which the school can deepen its relationship with the family. The second survey is designed to identify what home-based support each student has. Consider translating these surveys into the languages most used in your students' homes, sending them home in students' folders or passing them out at a parent or family event, or even bringing them to churches and local community organizations that your students' families frequently attend. Even if you do not have full participation from all parents or family members, you may learn some new information from those who do participate—which may help you to plan more effective ways to reach those who did not participate.

How to Use This Information

Like many written surveys, the one in Figure 10.2 asks for useful information but has a significant potential flaw: It is not accessible to family members with limited literacy or limited time to fill out surveys (or if it is not

Figure 10.2 Family Survey I (to be translated into the language spoken by family members)

We are always glad to see that our students are familiar with languages besides English. Please take a moment to share a little bit with us about your child's background:

What languages are spoken in your home?

In what language does your child feel most comfortable communicating?

In what language do you feel most comfortable communicating?

In what countries has your child gone to school?

For how long?

What other schools in the United States did your child attend?

For how long?

What would you like your child to learn about this year?

What are your child's favorite subjects?

(Continued)

Figure 10.2 (Continued)

Do you have a subject where you feel most comfortable helping your child? Are there subjects where you would like your child to receive help from other people (tutors or teachers)?

What would you like teachers to know about your child in order to help him or her learn?

What are the best days and times to reach you or your child's other parent or guardian?

What is the best way to reach you (phone, e-mail, or personal meeting)?

Have you been a parent or guardian in this school before?

Are you interested in volunteering in the school this year? (Yes or No)

What assistance can the school provide to you this year? Check all that apply:

_____ Weekly updates on class activities

_____ Extra material related to your child's academic learning

_____ Classes in the following areas:

_____ ESL

_____ Resume writing

_____ Job-interviewing skills

_____ Basic reading and writing

_____ Other; please suggest topics:

translated, to family members with limited English proficiency). In that case, this list may function more as a set of guiding questions, or information that you need to know to support students effectively. Consider asking some of these questions orally when you meet with parents at family nights; or if students have more literacy and English proficiency skills than family members, ask students to provide you some or all of the information after discussing the questions with parents or family members.

One school in our recent experience held a family forum, with interpreters and students present to translate for parents: Parents and other family members could come together to share their ideas about how to make the school more responsive to the linguistic and cultural needs of the student body. Topics such as those addressed in the survey could be part of the discussion at such an event.

Another and perhaps more ready-to-use survey is provided in Figure 10.3. The goal of this particular questionnaire is to identify the diverse literacy backgrounds of parents and family members in order to discover what kind of home-based support each child has. The teacher who designed this tool circulated at family events, such as the welcome-back picnic before school started, and on the first day of school, asking parents to respond orally rather than relying on those who returned a preprinted survey (particularly as her goal was to reach those family members who might not have well-developed literacy skills).

Sibling relationships can be a source of emotional strength—and academic support— for students.

How to Use This Information

This survey (see Figure 10.3) can be used as a stepping stone to identify appropriate methods of communicating with families, a tool to help teachers understand the home context in which students function, and a guide to help schools understand how to better support parents. However, it can also be used as a springboard to get to know families even better, through home visits, family events, and other family centered activities. This will allow families to be a part of the school community, share their stories, and also share the knowledge and strength that helps them to support their children.

Finding out more information about parents and family members is the first step toward creating positive relationships with them. However, it is also important to approach this information from a perspective of respect for families' cultural and academic backgrounds. The "funds of knowledge" approach (Gonzalez, Moll, & Amanti, 2005) is a good one to keep in mind here. In a

Figure 10.3   Family Survey II

Name: _____   Phone Number: _____

Child's Name: _____   Teacher's Name: _____

Welcome Back to School

Please take a moment to answer the following questions so that we can create programs that appropriately meet your needs this school year:

Section A

I am able to (check all that apply)

_____ Read books to my child in English

_____ Read books to my child in my native language (if it is not English)

_____ Call the front office to give and request information

_____ Fill out school forms written in English without assistance

_____ Easily communicate with school personnel (teachers, the principal, secretaries, etc.)

Section B

I would like help with (check all that apply)

_____ How to help my child with homework

_____ How to get support services for my child (health care, tutors, social services, etc.)

_____ How to use public transportation to attend school events with my child

_____ Receiving school documents in my own language

Section C

Please list any areas in which you think the school can provide you with help:

Source: Ayana Shabazz (2009). Used with permission.

funds of knowledge model, the diversity and richness of families' backgrounds is seen as an asset in the same way that academic skills might be. That diversity and richness may include intergenerational knowledge; humor; deeply held cultural traditions, values, and ethics; qualities such as resourcefulness and determination; and a close-knit sense of extended family and community. In a funds of knowledge approach, each of these is seen as a real asset, one that serves as a welcome source of strength for students and families (Gonzalez, Moll, & Amanti, 2005).

4. Be willing to reach out to families in new ways.

As in the vignette opening this chapter, we sometimes go through the motions without having the opportunity to question whether those motions are, in fact, the ones most likely to bring about change. Teachers and school administrators alike can think outside the box and design some innovative yet highly effective ways of making contact with families. For example, consider planning a family field trip as a way of making contact with those families who may be available on the weekend as opposed to the weekdays. One family coordinator whom we worked with designed a framework for a field trip held outside school hours (with the costs partially supported by the PTA and partially supported by a mini-grant) that would bring families, students, and teachers together to visit a local free museum. In this experience, the school provided continental breakfast before the event and also provided bus service (to cut costs, one could choose a location accessible via public transportation and ask participants to meet onsite). Supplementary enrichment materials, including assignments that called for students to discuss relevant topics with a family member, were designed and distributed in school before and after the trip. Assignments, directions, and activities can be provided in multiple languages; and bilingual parents or staff members can serve as guides for groups of families on the trip.

How to Use This Information

Each of the strategies in Figure 10.4 is a suggestion and, more important, a starting point. Based on what you have identified as your families' unique needs, some of these ideas may seem more or less appropriate to your population's needs. If in doubt about where to start, consider selecting one idea from the list; implement it on a limited basis (perhaps in one classroom) and track the results. If it seems to impact relationships with families in a positive way, consider adding some more steps or ideas the next month, or suggest some of the steps to colleagues if you find that they work for you.

5. Explore innovative ways to partner with community organizations to support families and their needs.

The idea of wraparound services has gained popularity in recent years (Blank, Jacobson, & Pearson, 2009). Schools can apply this concept to the area of

Figure 10.4	Innovative Ways to Reach Out to Family Members

Schools can create a community resource list providing names, contact information, and brief descriptions for local resources, social service agencies, and advocacy or education organizations. They can make it available in hard copy or online, in multiple languages.

Ask students (or teachers) to put together a booklet, series of posters, or even a short video depicting a "day in the life" of the school. Such a resource could be used to share information with families, who may not be familiar with school expectations, routines, and academic demands.

Ask students to work with their families to create a brochure, booklet, poster, or (if feasible) video depicting a day in the life of their family. Much like the school poster or video, such a project not only allows students to develop fine arts, critical thinking, and storytelling skills, but it also provides a way for students and families to make school staff aware of their backgrounds. Children and families can make heritage boxes containing artifacts that represent their heritage and background.

Students and families can also do a "heritage recording" using an audio or video recorder, recording a family member telling a story, videotaping a family event, or recording themselves discussing their heritage. Schools may wish to consider requesting support from a local merchant or foundation for purchasing cameras to lend to families.

Families can help children do family heritage timelines, using chart paper or sentence strips sent home from school. These, like the heritage box, would provide an opportunity for families to discuss their cultural background and heritage together and to identify particularly important events to be included on the timeline.

Families can record (or illustrate) their favorite fairy tale, poem, or song. The stories can be housed in the school media center or in each classroom. This activity, like the preceding ones, could easily be integrated into a language arts or social studies unit.

Schools can develop communication journals, using pictures as well as words (or in place of words), to document improvements or report concerns or accomplishments at home.

Rather than asking families to support the school financially, which may be difficult for families of diverse students, schools can request that families contribute time to refurbishing the school facilities: paint, clean, plant or replant, sand tables, sew curtains, do light construction, and other activities that help to maintain the physical plant.

To ensure all families are aware of the opportunities that are open to students at the school, school personnel can design and send a large postcard home with information about the extracurricular options. Consider putting the words "For Free," printed in different languages, on the postcard, and then including photos or graphics that illustrate the opportunities available in drama, music, sports, leadership positions, service, and other areas at the school. Consider including a contact number or e-mail address for a person who can put families in touch with the facilitator or coach for each activity.

Ask families where they would like to meet with school staff. Some families feel more comfortable meeting on neutral territory, or in other words, in a location where they feel safe: where authorities are not present and where they know they will not be asked for identification. Consider using a church center, community organization, or community room in a local housing complex.

family support by identifying family needs, contacting appropriate community organizations, and partnering with them to make resources available within the school (or with the school facilitating contact). As suggested in Chapter 7, consider establishing a family resource center that provides information within the school about local organizations and agencies. This could be as simple as a table or student desk in front of the office, featuring materials in several languages. You could also partner with agencies to provide support to students and families, to present at meetings, or to help connect students with needed resources. For example, some foundations will provide support for students' health-care needs, books for homes, and even shoes for athletic activities. Indeed, you may be saying, "That's great in theory, but who could I connect with, and what do I do once I connect with them?" The chart in Figure 10.5 may help you to brainstorm appropriate local or national agencies or organizations that could help, in addition to those suggested at the end of the chapter. Organized around the concept of Maslow's needs, the chart asks you to consider the varied needs of the "whole child" (Baca & Cervantes, 2004) and provides space to list community resources as you think of them. If you do not have the time or knowledge to fill out the chart yourself, consider passing it around before a department or faculty meeting—we guarantee that the collective knowledge of all your colleagues will go a long way toward filling it out!

Maslow's hierarchy (1943) states that individuals prioritize certain needs over other simultaneously existing needs in order to ensure basic survival. In the hierarchy, needs such as self-actualization, which may be met through education, work, or volunteer activities, take a secondary role to more basic needs such as food, shelter, and safety. In line with Baca and Cervantes's (2004) view of the whole child, we believe schools' approach to family and community involvement must address the needs of the whole child and, perhaps, even the "whole family," seeing individuals and families as more than simply the sum of their academic accomplishments and potential. Accordingly, this chart (see Figure 10.5) suggests ways that schools can partner with groups throughout the community to support families in addressing all of these needs that children may have. This chart, like Maslow's hierarchy, places basic needs at the bottom and more abstract needs at the top, identifying needs that may exist for students and families along various stages of Maslow's hierarchy.

How to Use This Information

As with other suggestions or steps provided in this book, no individual, committee, or school community can support all of these needs simultaneously—at least at the beginning. We recommend that you start, as Maslow did, with the basic needs. Identify what basic needs children and families at your school may exhibit, and review the suggested steps in Figure 10.5 to see what might be feasible in your school community. Choose one potential partner organization each month to which the school has not yet reached out, and spend the year trying to establish helpful partnerships and relationships. It may take a while. You may reach out to ten organizations and end up partnering with one or two, but those one or two will be worthwhile if you help to meet your students' and families' needs and support them in becoming available to learn.

Figure 10.5	Student and Family Needs, Steps to Support Them, and Potential Partner Organizations		

Needs of Students and Families	Organizations and Steps for Families	Organizations and Steps for Schools	Additional Community Resources Not Listed
Esteem and relationships with others; self-actualization and fulfillment	Family conversation groups, particularly those with an international focus; religious or spiritual institutions; community and special-interest groups; immigrant advocacy groups	School conversation groups; peer-to-peer support groups and mentoring; positive behavior and support initiatives; varied extracurricular activities that support a variety of student (and family) interests and needs	
Safety and security: emotional and mental	Mental wellness groups; counselors; family therapists at community centers or health clinics	School counselors and psychologists; positive behavior and support initiatives; character education initiatives	
Safety and security: physical	Shelters; community organizers and community advocacy organizations; immigrant advocacy and support groups	Collaborative relationships with law enforcement; community support initiatives; positive interventions for juveniles and those reentering society after incarceration	
Food	Food pantries; religious organizations and community assistance groups	Community organizations and assistance groups; social services; school lunch programs	
Shelter	Shelters; employment counseling and assistance organizations; religious organizations and neighborhood networks	Collaborative relationships with local shelters; support and planning to facilitate smooth transitions for students with high mobility due to housing or economic issues	

SUMMARY

There is an urgent need to involve families in the life of the school community, a need made more pressing because of what we now know about the diversity of families, backgrounds, languages, cultures, and lifestyles. There are numerous ways to approach this goal, but each method chosen must involve families as equal partners in the educational process, who have significant gifts to share and whose input is crucial to student success. This chapter reviews several approaches that schools may profitably take to increase family involvement. Each of these should begin by looking at families, assessing who they are and what their background might be, and should culminate with the identification of ways to enhance current efforts in order to involve families as fully as possible.

EXTENSION AND COLLABORATION

1. Consider teaming up with a colleague to host a joint family event at a time that is identified to be convenient for parents and family members. You could invite parents to school in the morning, before classes begin, for an informal coffee-and-doughnuts breakfast, for example. You may find, depending on the needs of your family population, that changing the time increases the percentage of parents who attend. On the other hand, it may not—the solution may be more complex.

2. If you do not have one already, team up with your grade-level or team colleagues to produce a weekly or monthly newsletter to send home to families. Your district may have support to translate the newsletter into multiple languages (or a bilingual colleague may be able to help as well). You can include updates about the class events, curriculum, student accomplishments, school events, and the like. Include a tear-off form at the bottom that parents can detach and send in if they have more questions to discuss with you.

3. Contact the staff at your cluster schools (including feeder schools, nearby schools on the same grade level). If you have a number of parents who are "common" to both schools, coordinate your family events so that families can attend both without having to prioritize one child's school experience over another.

NEXT STEPS

It is ironic that, as in so many other books in the field, our "family involvement" chapter comes at the end of the book. From the placement of this chapter, we realize the topic may appear to be an afterthought. However, we understand and strongly believe that, far from being an afterthought, family involvement is foundational to student success. The chapter is placed at the end of the book because it is difficult to appropriately and effectively reach out to families without understanding the full spectrum of linguistic, cultural, etiological, and academic dynamics that may impact not only students' success but also their families' well-being and relationship with the school.

There is no "next chapter" to link this final chapter to. Rather, we hope that you will see this chapter, and these suggestions, as a jumping-off point. This also represents a somewhat cyclical end to the book. Knowing what you now know about language, how has your picture of family communication changed? Knowing what you now know about family involvement and the challenges that schools may unwittingly put in the way of families seeking to support their children, how might your view of mental wellness, or students' behavior, change? The ideas presented here represent a small portion of the creative and welcoming ways that schools can choose to involve families of CLD students. Each of these suggestions, as we indicated at the beginning of the chapter, is rooted in the idea that the richness and strength of families' backgrounds should be acknowledged by schools and integrated into the ongoing "life" of the school community. This involves reaching out to parents; respecting differences of opinion that may arise with parents, whether they are based in language, culture, religion, socioeconomics, or other factors; and actively utilizing the diversity of students' backgrounds in day-to-day instruction as well as family events and activities.

COMMUNITY CONNECTIONS

1. Consider applying for outside support for your family outreach efforts. Local merchants may be willing to hand out flyers for school events or to make in-kind contributions of food, materials, or even funds. Your local chamber of commerce, philanthropic council, or other nonprofit organizations may have suggestions as to community-based grant resources that may be available. There are several larger organizations that also provide grants for schools to improve in areas such as family involvement (see Useful Websites on the following pages), but national grant competitions typically are more competitive and may involve more complex applications than that required by a local community organization. You may look into partnering with a longstanding existing organization: CEC (Council for Exceptional Children), National Council of La Raza (a national Latino advocacy group), or TESOL (teaching English to speakers of other languages). Often, university chapters of these organizations may be looking for community service projects and would be more than willing to work with your class or school to provide some support.

2. After conducting outreach efforts to get to know families better (which may include conversations, interviews, or the surveys provided earlier in the chapter), identify one or two community organizations that provide services from which the school's families could benefit. This may, for example, include ESOL instruction, help with resume writing or filling out job applications, and connections to medical insurance and care resources. Request that a representative from the organization attend the school's next parent night or HSA (Home and School Association) meeting, and promote the event among families.

3. If door-to-door visits are not practical (as they are not encouraged in many school districts), contact a local church, store, or agency where your students' families spend time. Spend an afternoon or two at that location, meeting and greeting families and also learning more about any resources provided at that site. You can share your new knowledge both with students and families and with colleagues at the school.

USEFUL WEBSITES

- Center on School, Family, and Community Partnerships: www.csos .jhu.edu/P2000/center.htm. This website, administered by faculty at Johns Hopkins University, conducts and disseminates research related to facilitation of family and community involvement in schools.
- Harvard Family Research Project: www.hfrp.org. This project, in existence for a number of years, provides information and research on family and school collaboration. The project's website contains links to current research, articles with ideas that may be useful for schools, links to publications, and summaries of information in specific areas (such as family involvement, out-of-school time, and complementary learning).
- National Parent Involvement Resource Center Coordination Center: www.nationalpirc.org. The U.S. Department of Education funds a number of Parent Involvement Resource Centers (PIRCs) around the country. This site provides a useful directory, a clearinghouse of information available from the centers, and guidance for school systems around the country seeking to maximize parent and family involvement.
- The SEDL National Center for Family and Community Connections With Schools: www.sedl.org/connections. SEDL, a private, nonprofit research and development organization, operates a center that has put toolkits and resources online, posts information about topics such as family involvement in Title I schools, and provides access to a large online collection of primary sources as well as syntheses of the literature on various topics.

References

Abedi, J. (2004, January/February). The No Child Left Behind Act and English language learners: Assessment and accountability issues. *Educational Researcher, 33*(1), 4–14.

Adkins, M. A., Sample, B., & Birman, D. (1999). *Mental health and the adult refugee: The role of the ESL teacher.* Washington, DC: National Clearinghouse for ESL Literacy Education. (ERIC Document Reproduction Service No. ED439625)

American Psychological Association. (2003). *Addressing missed opportunities for early childhood mental health intervention: Current knowledge and policy implications: Report of the Task Force on Early Mental Health Intervention.* Retrieved from www.apa.org/pi/families/resources/early-mental-health.pdf

Americans with Disabilities Act of 1990, Public Law No. 101–336, § 2, 104 Stat. 328 (1991).

Armstrong, T. (2000). *Multiple intelligences in the classroom.* Alexandria, VA: ASCD.

Artiles, A. (2003). Special education's changing identity: Paradoxes and dilemmas in views of culture and space. *Harvard Educational Review, 73*(2), 164. Retrieved from Academic Search Premier database

August, D., & Shanahan, T. (Eds.). (2006). *Executive summary: Developing literacy in second-language learners: Report of the National Literacy Panel on Language-Minority Children and Youth.* Mahwah, NJ: Lawrence Erlbaum.

Baca, L., & Cervantes, H. (2004). *The bilingual special education interface* (4th ed.). Upper Saddle River, NJ: Prentice Hall.

Baca, L. M., & de Valenzuela, J. S. (2004). Background and rationale for bilingual special education. In L. M. Baca & H. T. Cervantes, *The bilingual special education interface* (4th ed.). Upper Saddle River, NJ: Prentice Hall.

Barbassa, J. (2007, April 3). Children face difficult decision when immigrant parents deported. *Associated Press.* Retrieved from www.miracoalition.org/press/general-news/federal-officials-in-immigrant-raid-decline-to-appear-before-legislative-committee?func=previousThread

Batalova, J. (2006). *Spotlight on legal immigration to the United States.* Migration Policy Institute, Washington, DC. Retrieved June 1, 2010 from http://www.migrationinformation.org/Feature/display.cfm?ID=414#2

Blank, M., Jacobson, R., & Pearson, S. (2009). A coordinated effort: Well-conducted partnerships meet students' academic, health, and social service needs. *American Educator, 33*(2), 30–36.

Boethel, M. (2004). *Readiness: School, family and community connections.* Austin, TX: Southwest Regional Educational Laboratory.

Broekhuizen, D. (2004). English language learners: Who are they? *Pacific Educator, 3*(3), 4.

Buttaro, L. (2002, February). Second language acquisition, culture shock and language stress of adult Latina students in New York. In *An imperfect world: Resonance from the nation's violence* (2002 Monograph Series). Proceedings of the Annual Meeting of the National Association of African American Studies, the National Association of Hispanic and Latino Studies, the National Association of Native American Studies, and the International Association of Asian Studies, Houston, TX.

Castañeda v. Pickard, 574 F.2d 268, 270 (5th Cir. 1978).

Centers for Medicare and Medicaid Services. (2009). *Children's Health Insurance Program: National CHIP policy.* Retrieved from www.cms.hhs.gov/home/chip.asp

Central Intelligence Agency. (2009). *The world factbook.* Retrieved Oct. 4, 2009, from www.cia.gov/library/publications/the-world-factbook/fields/2103.html

Chamot, A. (2009). *The CALLA handbook: Implementing the cognitive academic language learning approach.* Upper Saddle River, NJ: Pearson.

Clay, M. (1979). *The early detection of reading difficulties.* Portsmouth, NH: Heinemann.

Collier, C. (2010). *Seven steps to separating difference from disability.* Thousand Oaks, CA: Corwin.

Congressional Budget Office. (2006). *Immigration policy in the United States.* Washington, DC: Author.

Council for Exceptional Children. (2007, April 5). *CEC gives cautious approval to new regulations on assessing students with disabilities* [Press release]. Arlington, VA: Author.

Council of Chief State School Officers. (2009). *Annual survey of state student assessment programs, 2001–2002.* Washington, DC: Author.

Crotty, M. (1998). *The foundations of social research: Meaning and perspective in the research process.* Thousand Oaks, CA: Sage.

Cummins, J. (1981). The role of primary language development in promoting educational success for language minority students. In Bilingual Education Office (Ed.), *Schooling and language-minority students: A theoretical framework* (pp. 3–47). Los Angeles: Evaluation, Dissemination and Assessment Center, California State University.

Cummins, J. (2007). *BICS and CALP: Clarifying the distinction.* Retrieved from http://iteachilearn.com/cummins/bicscalp.html

Day, J., McDonnell, A., & Heathfield, L. (2005). Enhancing emergent literacy skills in inclusive preschools for young children with visual impairments. *Young Exceptional Children, 9*(1), 20–28.

Derwing, T. M. (2003). What do ESL students say about their accents? *Canadian Modern Language Review, 59,* 545–564.

Downey, D. B. (2002). Parental and family involvement in education. In A. Molnar (Ed.), *School reform proposals: The research evidence.* Charlotte, NC: Information Age.

Elley, W., & Mangubhai, F. (1983). The impact of reading on second language learning. *Reading Research Quarterly, 19*(1), 53–67.

Epstein, J. L., & Sanders, M. G. (2000). Connecting home, school, and community: New directions for social research. In M. T. Hallinan (Ed.), *Handbook of the sociology of education* (pp. 285–306). New York: Kluwer Academic/Plenum.

Ferguson, S. (2007). *Libraries in the twenty-first century: Charting new directions in information services* (Topics in Australasian Library and Information Studies No. 27). Wagga Wagga, Australia: Centre for Information Studies.

Frattura, E., & Capper, C. (2006, November). Segregated programs versus integrated comprehensive service delivery for all learners: Assessing the differences. *Remedial & Special Education, 27*(6), 355–364. Retrieved from Academic Search Premier database.

Freire, P. (1993). *Pedagogy of the oppressed.* New York: Herder & Herder.

Freire, P., & Macedo, D. (1987). *Literacy: Reading the word and the world.* South Hadley, MA: Bergin & Garvey.

Gardner, H. (2000). *Intelligence reframed: Multiple intelligences for the 21st century.* New York: Basic Books.

Gee, J. (2000). The new literacy studies: From "socially situated" to the work of the social. In D. Barton, M. Hamilton, & R. Ivanič (Eds.), *Situated literacies: Reading and writing in context* (pp. 177–194). New York: Routledge.

Genesee, F., Lindholm-Leary, K., Saunders, W. M., & Christian, D. (Eds.). (2006). *Educating English language learners: A synthesis of research evidence.* London: Cambridge University Press.

Godemann, J. (2008). Knowledge integration: a key challenge for transdisciplinary cooperation. *Environmental Education Research, 14*(6), 625–641.

Gonzalez. N., Moll, L., & Amanti, C. (Eds.). (2005). *Funds of knowledge: Theorizing practices in households, communities, and classrooms.* Mahwah, NJ: Lawrence Erlbaum.

Hakuta, K. (2007, February 12). *Castañeda v. Pickard (1981), LAU: A resource for students, teachers, researchers, and policymakers [1].* Stanford University School of Education. Retrieved from http://faculty.ucmerced.edu/khakuta/LAU/IAPolicy/IA1bCastanedaFullText.htm

Hanley, J. (1999). Beyond the tip of the iceberg: Five stages toward cultural competence. *Today's Youth: The Community Circle of Caring Journal, 3*(2), 9–12.

Harry, B. (2008). Collaboration with culturally and linguistically diverse families: Ideal versus reality. *Exceptional Children, 74*(3), 372–388. Retrieved from Academic Search Premier database

Henderson, A. T., & Berla, N. (Eds.). (1994). *A new generation of evidence: The family is critical to student achievement.* Washington, DC: National Committee for Citizens in Education. (ERIC Document Reproduction Service No. ED375968)

Henderson, A. T., & Mapp, K. L. (2002). *A new wave of evidence: The impact of school, family, and community connections on student achievement.* Retrieved from www.sedl.org/connections/resources/evidence.pdf

Herrera, S. G., & Murry, K. G. (2006). *Mastering ESL and bilingual methods.* Upper Saddle River, NJ: Pearson.

Hoover, J., Klingner, J., Baca, L., & Patton, J. (2008). *Methods for teaching culturally and linguistically diverse exceptional learners.* Upper Saddle River, NJ: Prentice Hall.

Individuals With Disabilities Improvement Act of 2004, Public Law No. 108–446 118 Stat. 2647 (2004).

Institute of Education Sciences. (2007). *Intervention ratings for beginning reading.* Retrieved from http://ies.ed.gov/ncee/wwc/reports/beginning_reading/topic/rating.asp

International Reading Association. (2009). *Getting your child ready to read.* Retrieved from www.reading.org/Libraries/Parents/pb1070_ready.sflb.ashx

International Reading Association & National Association for the Education of Young Children. (1998). *Learning to read and write: Developmentally appropriate practices for young children.* Washington, DC: National Association for the Education of Young Children.

Isserlis, J. (2000). *Trauma and the adult English language learner.* Washington, DC: National Clearinghouse for ESL Literacy Education. (ERIC Document Reproduction Service No. ED444397)

Johnson, D., & Sulzby, E. (1999). *Critical issue: Addressing the literacy needs of emergent and early readers.* Retrieved from www.ncrel.org/sdrs/areas/issues/content/cntareas/reading/li100.htm

Johnson, E., Mellard, D. F., Fuchs, D., & McKnight, M. A. (2006). *Responsiveness to intervention (RTI): How to do it.* Lawrence, KS: National Research Center on Learning Disabilities.

Kennedy, J. F. (2004). *Profiles in courage* (Anniversary ed.). New York: HarperCollins.

Kindler, A. (2002). *Survey of the states' limited English proficient students and available educational program and services 2000–2001 summary report.* Washington, DC: National Clearinghouse for English Language Acquisition.

Klingner, J. K., Artiles, A. J., Kozleski, E., Harry, B., Zion, S., Tate, W., et al. (2005). Addressing the disproportionate representation of culturally and linguistically diverse students in special education through culturally responsive educational systems. *Education Policy Analysis Archives, 13*(38).

Kohl, H. (2002). Topsy-turvies: Teacher talk and student talk. In L. Delpit & J. Dowdy (Eds.), *The skin that we speak: Thoughts on language and culture in the classroom* (pp. 145–162). New York: New Press.

Kuder, S., & Hasit, C. (2002). *Enhancing literacy for all students.* Upper Saddle River: Prentice Hall.

Lau v. Nichols, 414 U.S. 563 (1974).

Lopez-Reina, N. (1996). The importance of meaningful contexts in bilingual special education: Moving to whole language. *Learning Disabilities Research and Practice, 11,* 120–131.

Losardo, A., & Notari-Syverson, A. (2001). *Alternative approaches to assessing young children.* Baltimore: Paul H. Brookes.

Lotan, R. (2006). Teaching teachers to build equitable classrooms. *Theory Into Practice, 45*(1), 32–39.

Maslow, A. (1943). A theory of human motivation. *Psychological Review, 50*(4), 370–396.

Mason, J. L. (1993). *Cultural competence self-assessment questionnaire.* Portland, OR: Portland State University.

Mazur, A., & Givens, S. (2004, May/June). The impact of mental health on school success of ELLs: To refer or not? *NABE News,* pp. 10–14.

Moll, L. (1994). Literacy research in community and classrooms: A sociocultural approach. In R. R. Ruddel, M. R. Ruddell, & H. Singer (Eds.), *Theoretical models and processes of reading* (4th ed., pp. 179–207). Newark, DE: International Reading Association.

National Association of School Psychologists. (2009). *Supporting children's mental health: Tips for parents and educators.* Rockville, MD: Author. Retrieved from www.nasponline.org/resources/mentalhealth/mhtips.aspx

National Center for Children in Poverty. (2003). *Low-income children in the United States.* Retrieved from www.gettingready.org/matriarch/MultiPiecePage.asp_Q_PageID_E_212_A_PageName_E_FamilyCommunEnironments

National Clearinghouse for English Language Acquisition. (2006). *Types of language instruction educational programs.* Retrieved from www.ncela.gwu.edu/files/uploads/5/Language_Instruction_Educational_Programs.pdf

National Clearinghouse for English Language Acquisition. (2008). *National and regional data and demographics.* Retrieved from www.ncela.gwu.edu/stats/2_nation.htm

National Clearinghouse for English Language Acquisition. (2009). *Accountability.* Retrieved from www.ncela.gwu.edu/accountability

National Education Association. (2007). *Truth in labeling: Disproportionality in special education.* Washington, DC: Author.

National Education Association. (2009). *Voices from the classroom: NCLB stories.* Retrieved Sept. 24, 2009, from www.nea.org/home/1256.htm

National Institute for Literacy. (2007). *What content-area teachers should know about adolescent literacy.* Retrieved from www.nifl.gov/publications/pdf/adolescent_literacy07.pdf

National Institute for Literacy. (2009). *Definition of literacy.* Retrieved from www.nifl.gov/about/definition.html

National Reading Panel. (2000). *Teaching children to read: An evidence-based assessment of the scientific research literature on reading and its implications for reading instruction.* Available from www.nichd.nih.gov/publications/nrp/report.cfm

Neufeld, S. (2009, February 9). Pushing hard, with no excuses. *Baltimore Sun.* Retrieved from www.baltimoresun.com/news/education/balte.alonso09feb09,0,4438388, full.story

Nichols, M., & Schwartz, R. (2004). *Family therapy: Concepts and methods.* Upper Saddle River, NJ: Pearson.

No Child Left Behind Act of 2001, Public Law No. 107–110, 20 U.S.C. § 6301 et seq. (2002).

Nock, M. K., & Kurtz, S. M. S. (2005). Direct behavioral observation in school settings: Bringing science to practice. *Cognitive and Behavioral Practice, 12,* 359–370.

Obama, B. (2009, September 8). *Remarks by the President in a national address to America's schoolchildren, Wakefield High School, Arlington, VA.* Washington, DC: The White House.

Office of Special Education Programs. (2004). *Individuals With Disabilities Improvement Act of 2004.* Washington, DC: Author.

Office of Special Education Programs. (2006). *Guidance on IDEA.* Washington, DC: Author.

Páez, M., Tabors, P., & López, L. (2007). Dual language and literacy development of Spanish-speaking preschool children. *Journal of Applied Developmental Psychology, 28*(2), 85–102.

Parker, D. (1985). *Sheltered English: Theory to practice.* Paper presented at in-service workshop. San Diego, CA.

Pennock-Roman, M., & Rivera, C. (2007, September). *Test validity and mean effects of test accommodations for ELLs and non-ELLs: A meta-analysis* (Reidy Interactive Lecture Series). Retrieved from www.nciea.org/publications/RILS_MRCR07.pdf

Peregoy, S., & Boyle, O. (2008). *Reading, writing and learning in ESL* (5th ed.). Boston: Allyn & Bacon.

Perry, L. A. (1997). Using wordless picture books with beginning readers (of any age). *Teaching Exceptional Children, 29*(3), 68–69.

Polacco, P. (2001). *The Keeping Quilt.* New York: Aladdin.

Purcell-Gates, V. (1996). Stories, coupons, and the TV Guide: Relationships between home literacy experiences and emergent literacy knowledge. *Reading Research Quarterly, 31*(4), 406–428.

Rehabilitation Act of 1973, Public Law No. 93–112, 87 Stat. 394 (1973).

Reynolds, C., Livingston, R., & Willson, V. (2009). *Measurement and assessment in education* (2nd ed.). Boston: Allyn & Bacon.

Rueda, R., & Chan, K. (1979). Poverty and culture in special education: Separate but equal. *Exceptional Children, 45* (7), 422–431.

Rumelhart, D. E. (2004). Toward an interactive model of reading. In R. B. Ruddell & N. J. Unrau (Eds.), *Theoretical models and processes of reading.* Washington, DC: International Reading Association.

Sadker, D., & Sadker, M. (1988). *The intellectual exchange: Excellence and equity in college teaching.* Washington, DC: American University.

Sheldon, S. B. (2003). Linking school-family-community partnerships in urban elementary schools to student achievement on state tests. *Urban Review, 35*(2), 149–165.

Snow, C., Barnes, W., Chandler, J., Goodman, I., & Hemphill, L. (1991). *Unfulfilled expectations: Home and school influences on literacy.* Cambridge, MA: Harvard University Press.

Stiggins, R. J., & Conklin, N. F. (1992). *In teachers' hands: Investigating the practices of classroom assessment.* Albany: State University of New York Press.

Sulzby, E., & Teale, W. H. (1991). Emergent literacy. In R. Barr, M. L. Kamil, P. Mosenthal, & P. D. Pearson (Eds.), *Handbook of reading research* (pp. 727–757). New York: Longman.

Taylor, O. (1990). Culture, communication, and language. In *Cross-cultural communication: An essential dimension of effective education.* Retrieved from www.maec.org/cross/4.html

Taylor, R. (2009). *Assessment of exceptional students.* Upper Saddle River, NJ: Merrill.

Thoman, E., & Jolls, T. (2004). *Media literacy: A national priority for a changing world.* Retrieved from www.medialit.org/reading_room/article663.html

Thomas, W. P., & Collier, V. P. (2002). *A national study of school effectiveness for language minority students' long-term academic achievement.* Santa Cruz: Center for Research on Education, Diversity and Excellence, University of California.

United Nations Educational, Scientific and Cultural Organization Education Sector. (2004). *The plurality of literacy and its implications for policies and programs* [Position paper]. Retrieved from http://unesdoc.unesco.org/images/0013/001362/136246e.pdf

U.S. Department of Education. (2006). *The Secretary's fifth annual report on teacher quality: A highly qualified teacher in every classroom.* Washington, DC: Author.

U.S. Department of Education, National Center for Education Statistics. (2008). *Fast facts: How many students with disabilities receive services?* Available from http://nces .ed.gov/fastfacts

U.S. Department of Health and Human Services. (1999). *Mental health: A report of the Surgeon General: Executive summary.* Rockville, MD: Author.

U.S. Department of Health and Human Services. (2007). *About TANF.* Retrieved from www.acf.hhs.gov/programs/ofa/tanf/about.html

VanDerHeyden, A. M. (2008). Using RTI to accomplish system change. *ABAI Newsletter, 31*(3). Retrieved from www.abainternational.org/ABA/newsletter/vol313/ VanDerHeyden.asp

VanDerHeyden, A. M., Witt, J. C., & Gilbertson, D. A. (2007). Multi-year evaluation of the effects of a response to intervention (RTI) model on identification of children for special education. *Journal of School Psychology, 45,* 225–256.

Vygotsky, L. (1978). Interaction between learning and development. In M. Cole (Trans.), *Mind in society* (pp. 79–91). Cambridge, MA: Harvard University Press.

Xu, Y., & Drame, E. (2008). Culturally appropriate context: Unlocking the potential of response to intervention for English language learners. *Early Childhood Education Journal, 35*(4), 305–311.

Index

CORWIN
A SAGE Company

The Corwin logo—a raven striding across an open book—represents the union of courage and learning. Corwin is committed to improving education for all learners by publishing books and other professional development resources for those serving the field of PreK–12 education. By providing practical, hands-on materials, Corwin continues to carry out the promise of its motto: **"Helping Educators Do Their Work Better."**